Student Activity Journal

ACCESS

Building Literacy Through Learning™

Science

Great Source Education Group

a division of Houghton Mifflin Company

Wilmington, Massachusetts

www.greatsource.com

AUTHORS

Dr. Elva Duran holds a Ph.D. from the University of Oregon in special education and reading disabilities. Duran has been an elementary reading and middle school teacher in Texas and overseas. Currently, she is a professor in the Department of Special Education, Rehabilitation, and School Psychology at California State University, Sacramento, where she teaches beginning reading and language and literacy courses. Duran is co-author of the Leamos Español reading program and has published two textbooks, *Teaching Students with Moderate/Severe Disabilities* and *Systematic Instruction in Reading for Spanish-Speaking Students.*

Jo Gusman grew up in a family of migrants and knows firsthand the complexities surrounding a second-language learner. Gusman's career in bilingual education began in 1974. In 1981, she joined the staff of the Newcomer School in Sacramento. There she developed her brain-based ESL strategies. Her work has garnered national television appearances and awards, including the Presidential Recognition for Excellence in Teaching. Gusman is the author of *Practical Strategies for Accelerating the Literacy Skills and Content Learning of Your ESL Students.* She is a featured video presenter, including "Multiple Intelligences and the Second Language Learner." Currently, she teaches at California State University, Sacramento, and at the Multiple Intelligences Institute at the University of California, Riverside.

Dr. John Shefelbine is a professor in the Department of Teacher Education, California State University, Sacramento. His degrees include a Master of Arts in Teaching in reading and language arts, K-12, from Harvard University and a Ph.D. in educational psychology from Stanford University. During his 11 years as an elementary and middle school teacher, Shefelbine has worked with students from linguistically and culturally diverse populations in Alaska, Arizona, Idaho, and New Mexico. Shefelbine was a contributor to the California Reading Language Arts Framework, the California Reading Initiative, and the California Reading and Literature Project, and has authored a variety of reading materials and programs for developing fluent, confident readers.

EDITORIAL: Developed by Nieman Inc. with Phil LaLeike
DESIGN: Ronan Design

Printed in the United States of America

International Standard Book Number -13: 978-0-669-50901-4
International Standard Book Number -10: 0-669-50901-9
(*Student Activity Journal*)

5 6 7 8 9—P00—10 09 08 07 06

International Standard Book Number -13: 978-0-669-51660-9
International Standard Book Number -10: 0-669-51660-0
(*Student Activity Journal, Teacher's Edition*)

3 4 5 6 7 8 9—P00—10 09 08 07 06 05

CONSULTANTS

Shane Bassett
Mill Park Elementary School
David Douglas School District
Portland, OR

Jeanette Gordon
Senior Educational Consultant
Illinois Resource Center
Des Plaines, IL

Dr. Aixa Perez-Prado
College of Education
Florida International University
Miami, FL

Dennis Terdy
Director of Grants and Special Programs
Newcomer Center
Township High School
Arlington Heights, IL

TEACHER GROUP REVIEWERS

Sara Ainsworth
Hannah Beardsley Middle School
Crystal Lake, IL

Walter A. Blair
Otis Elementary School
Chicago, IL

Vincent U. Egonmwan
Joyce Kilmer Elementary School
Chicago, IL

Anne Hopkins
Arie Crown School
Skokie, IL

Heather Pusich
Field Middle School
Northbrook, IL

Dana Robinson
Prairie Crossing Charter School
Grayslake, IL

Nestor Torres
Chase Elementary School
Chicago, IL

RESEARCH SITE LEADERS

Carmen Concepción
Lawton Chiles Middle School
Miami, FL

Andrea Dabbs
Edendale Middle School
San Lorenzo, CA

Daniel Garcia
Public School 130
Bronx, NY

Bobbi Ciriza Houtchens
Arroyo Valley High School
San Bernardino, CA

Portia McFarland
Wendell Phillips High School
Chicago, IL

RESEARCH SITE SCIENCE REVIEWERS

Kristen Can
Edendale Middle School
San Lorenzo, CA

Delores King
Warren Elementary School
Chicago, IL

Dania E. Lima
Lawton Chiles Middle School
Miami, FL

Elizabeth Tremberger
Bronx, NY

Jackie Womack
Martin Luther King, Jr. Middle School
San Bernardino, CA

SCIENCE TEACHER REVIEWERS

Said Salah Ahmed
Sanford Middle School
Minneapolis, MN

Kellie A. Danzinger
Carpentersville Middle School
Carpentersville, IL

Jean E. Garrity
Washington Middle School
Kenosha, WI

Jon L. Kimsey
Carpenter Elementary School
Chicago, IL

Anna Kong
Stone Academy
Chicago, IL

Jill McCarthy
Auburndale, MA

Donna O'Neill
Luther Jackson Middle School
Falls Church, VA

Kevin Smith
North Welcome Center
Columbus, OH

Nancy Svendsen
J. E. B. Stuart School
Falls Church, VA

Jill M. Thompson
Roosevelt Middle School
Blaine, MN

ACKNOWLEDGMENTS
Cover Credits: *Foreground*: frog: © Getty Images; prism: © Getty Images; stars: © Photodisc/Getty Images *Background:* © Photodisc/Getty Images; © BrandX/Getty Images. Based on a system of labeling the columns A through J and the rows 1 through 18, the following background images were taken by the following photographers: A8, A10, A13, A16, A18, C9, C11, C13, C14, C16, C17, D5, D7, D8, D11, D13, D15, D18, E1, E8, E12, E15, E16, E17, E19, E20, F1, F2, F5, F6, F11, F13, F17, F19, G9, G10, G12, H2, H3, H12, H13, H17, I1, I8, I9, I11, I14, I16, I18, I19, J2, J4, J5, J6, J8, J12, J13, J17, J19: Philip Coblentz/Getty Images; A5, E7: Steve Allen/Getty Images; F16: Sexto Sol/Getty Images; B19: Spike Mafford/Getty Images; B12: Philippe Colombi/Getty Images; J1: Albert J Copley/Getty Images
Photo Credits: 4 *top* © Eileen Ryan Photography, 2004 *center right* © Royalty-Free/CORBIS *bottom* © Eileen Ryan Photography, 2004 **5** *top* © Getty Images *center right* © Eileen Ryan Photography, 2004 *bottom* © Eileen Ryan Photography, 2004 **104** © Charles D. Winters/Photo Researchers, Inc. **105** © Getty Images **106** © Eileen Ryan Photography, 2004 **107** © Royalty-Free/CORBIS **108** © Eileen Ryan Photography, 2004 **110** © Getty Images
Illustration Credits: 96 © Jonathan Massie

TABLE OF

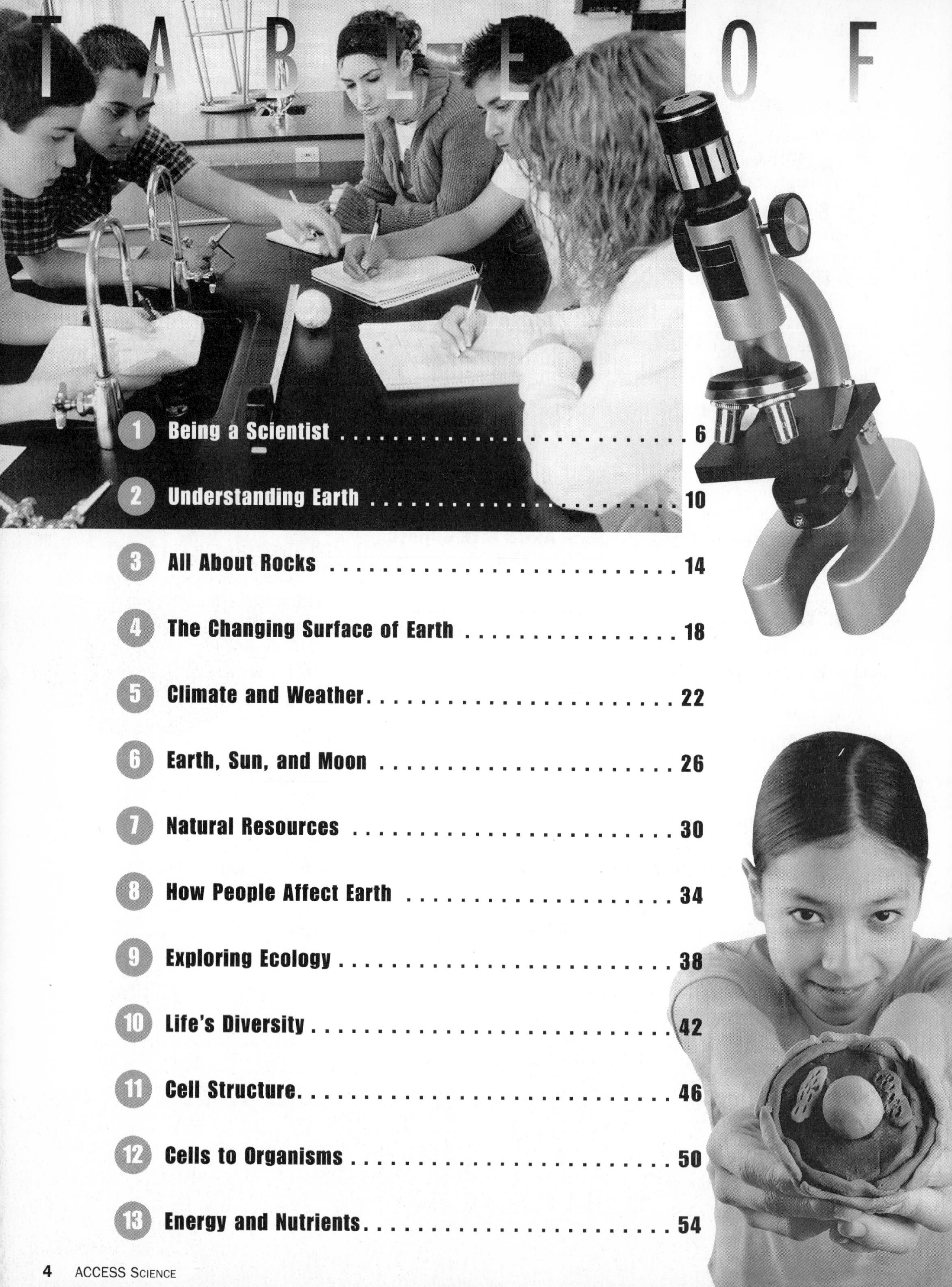

CONTENTS

Name ____________________

Being a Scientist

My Word List

A. Word Web As you study Lesson 1 in *ACCESS Science*, complete the Word Web below with vocabulary words from the lesson. In the ovals, write words that describe parts of the science process.

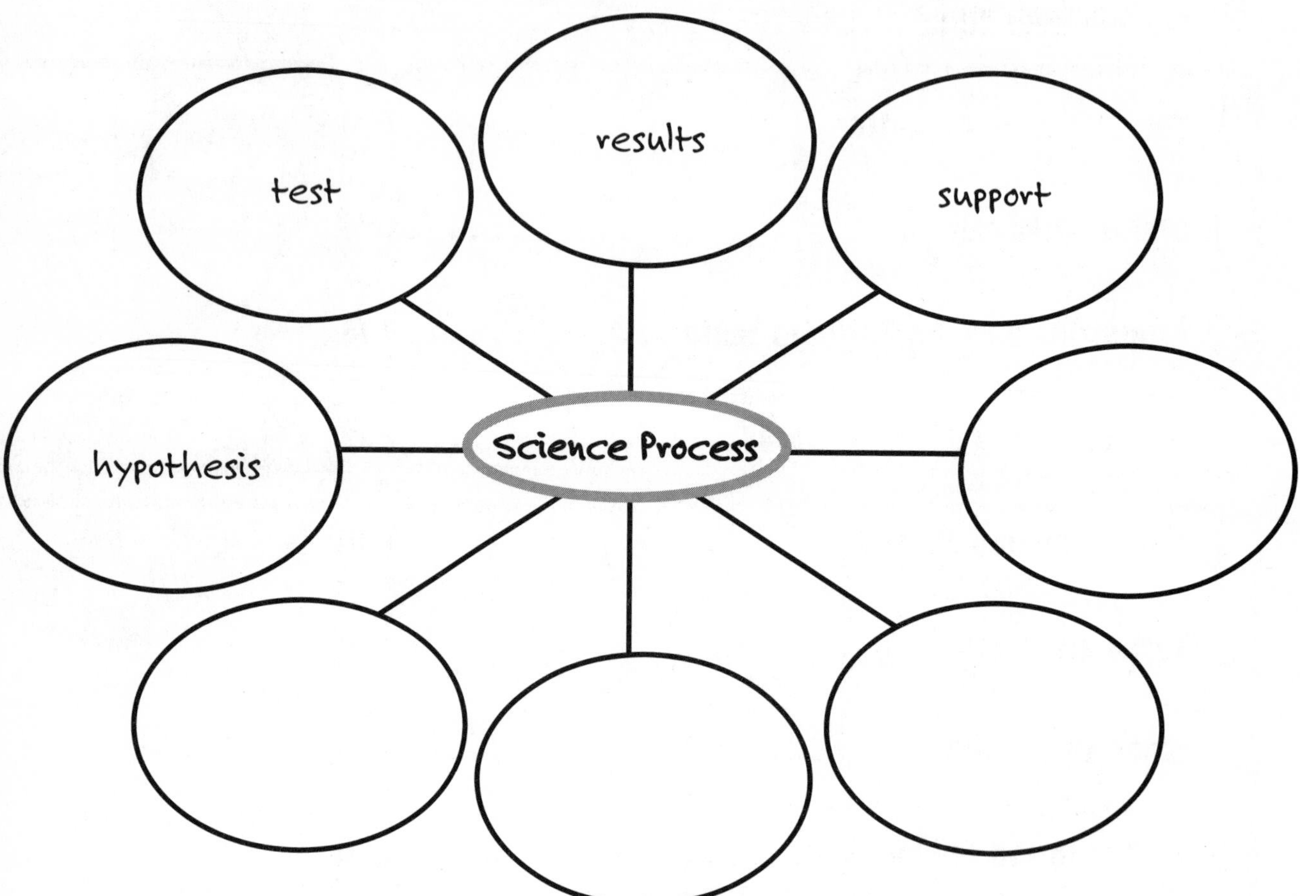

B. Writing Sentences Write 2–3 sentences describing how parts of the science process relate to one another. Use at least 3 words from your Word Web.

____

____

____

____

____

Name ______________________

FOR USE WITH PAGE 19

Skill Building

A. Use the Science Process After you study the lesson, use the space below to draw the steps of the bouncing ball experiment in order. Use the information on page 19. Then use your pictures to explain the experiment to a partner.

B. Choosing Vocabulary In each sentence below, underline the word that best completes the sentence.

1. I use my (explanations, senses) to observe the world.

2. (Variables, Results) are things that can affect what happens in an experiment.

3. Many times, (survey, technology) makes work easier.

4. I need to (support, analyze) my data before I can write a conclusion.

5. If scientists don't (communicate, affect), they cannot ask new questions.

Name

My Study Notes

A. Study Skill: Using Process Notes Complete the Process Notes for Lesson 1. Use information under each heading in *ACCESS Science* to write notes in the boxes.

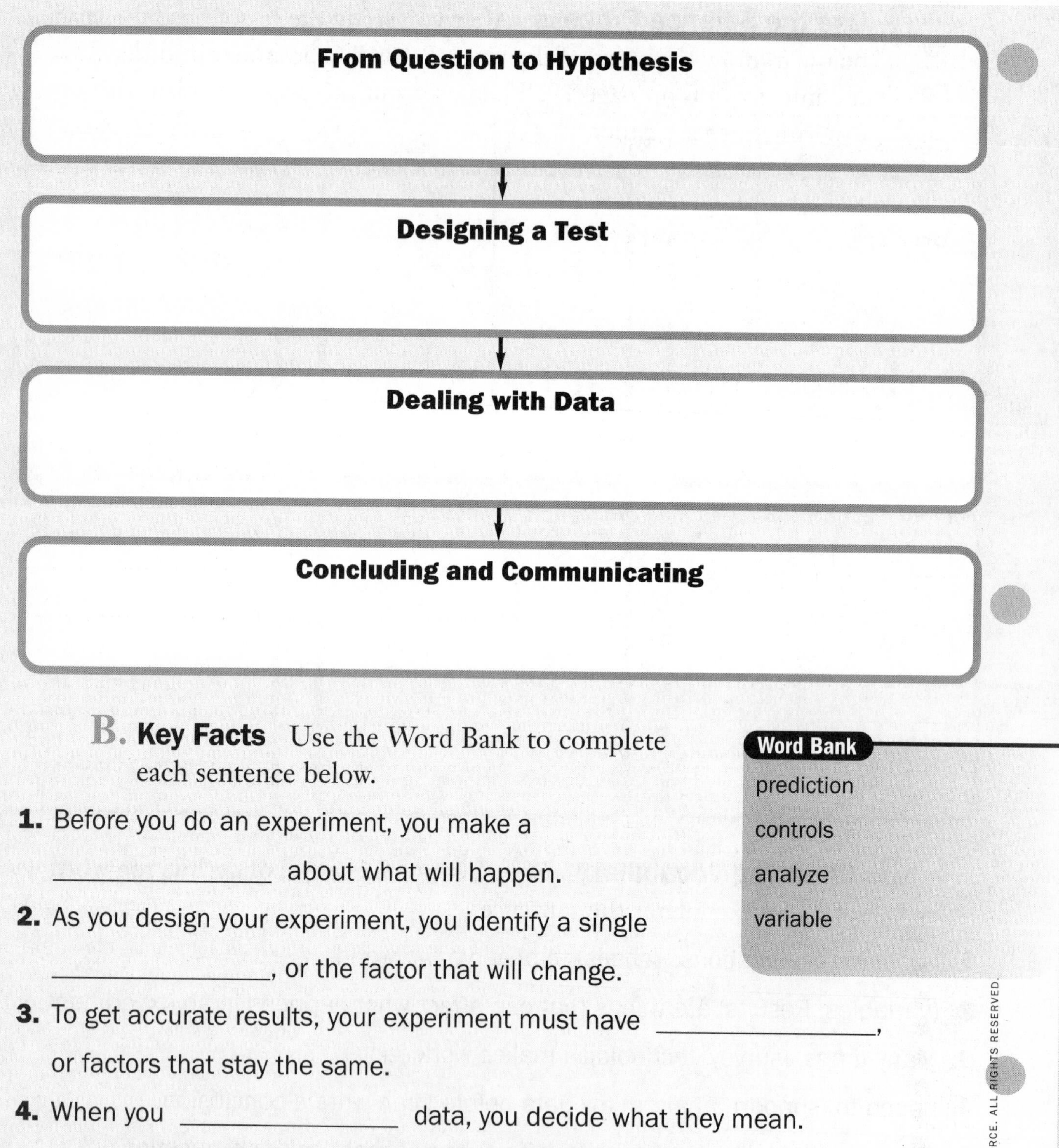

B. Key Facts Use the Word Bank to complete each sentence below.

Word Bank
- prediction
- controls
- analyze
- variable

1. Before you do an experiment, you make a ________________ about what will happen.

2. As you design your experiment, you identify a single ________________, or the factor that will change.

3. To get accurate results, your experiment must have ________________, or factors that stay the same.

4. When you ________________ data, you decide what they mean.

Name

FOR USE WITH PAGE 26

Showing What I Know

Relating Kim conducted an experiment to test this hypothesis: *Jackie will eat cheese faster than broccoli.* Think about the evidence in the chart below. Then write a possible explanation.

Evidence		Explanation
Food	**Eating Speed**	
cheese	10 minutes	
broccoli	5 minutes	

Think about the organizer above and then write 1–3 sentences to relate the evidence and your explanation. Be sure to say whether or not the results support the hypothesis.

My Summary of the Lesson

Name

Understanding Earth

My Word List

A. Definition Web Complete this Definition Web about the structure of Earth. Write the meaning of each word in the box.

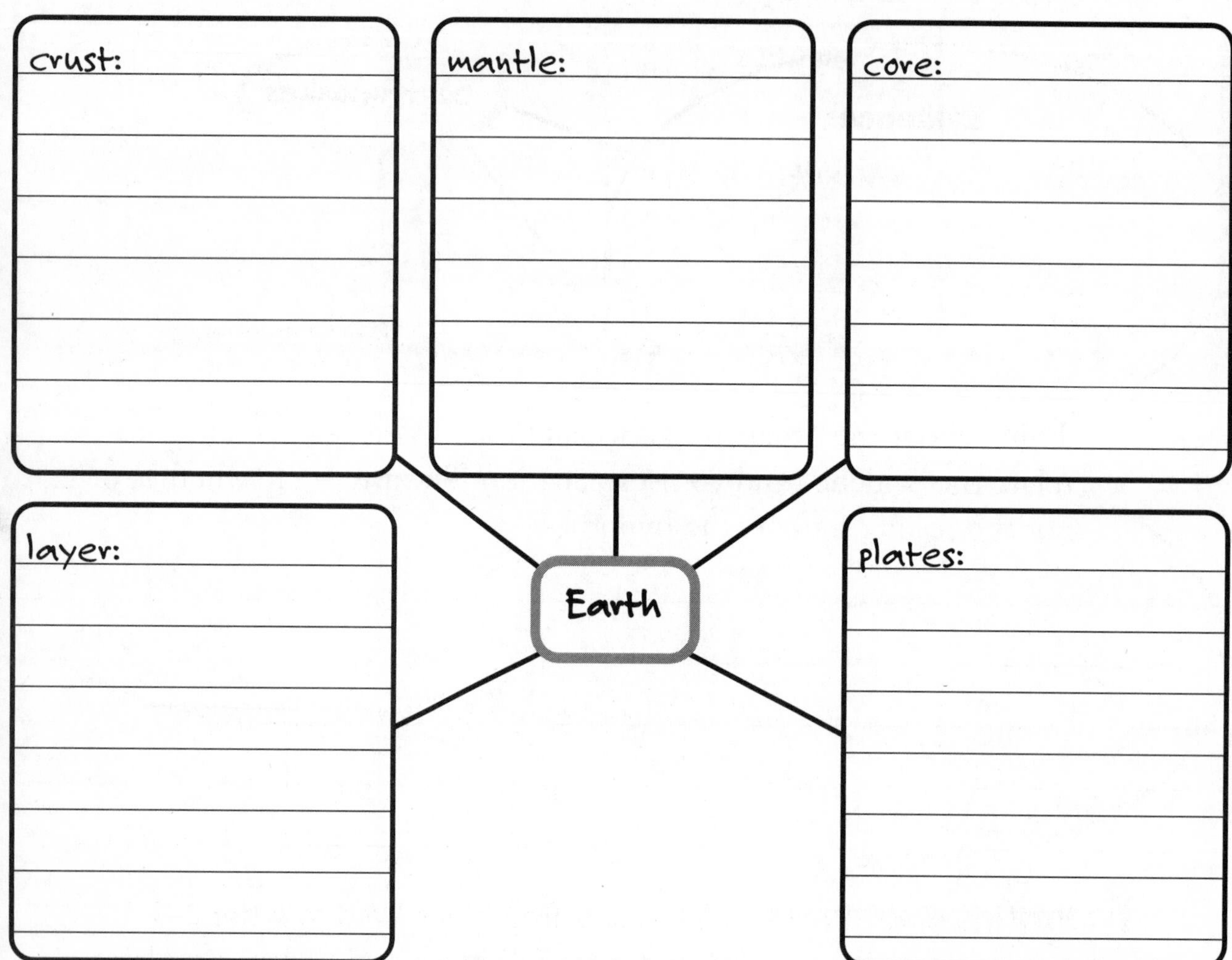

B. Sentence Frame Use the words in your Definition Web to complete the paragraph below.

Earth has 3 main layers. We live on the top ______________. This outside layer, with the oceans and continents, is called the ______________. Underneath the oceans and continents are ______________ that move. The thick middle layer of Earth is the ______________. The hot center of Earth is the ______________.

Name

FOR USE WITH PAGE 31

Skill Building

A. Analyze Evidence After you read the lesson, fill in this Web about earthquakes. In each oval, write one piece of evidence showing how earthquakes happen.

B. Writing Sentences Use details from your Web to write 2–3 sentences analyzing your evidence. Tell how your evidence explains why the ground shakes during an earthquake.

Name

My Study Notes

A. Study Skill: Using a Cause-Effect Organizer As you study the lesson, complete this Cause-Effect Organizer about plate tectonics. In the boxes, write 3 effects caused by moving plates.

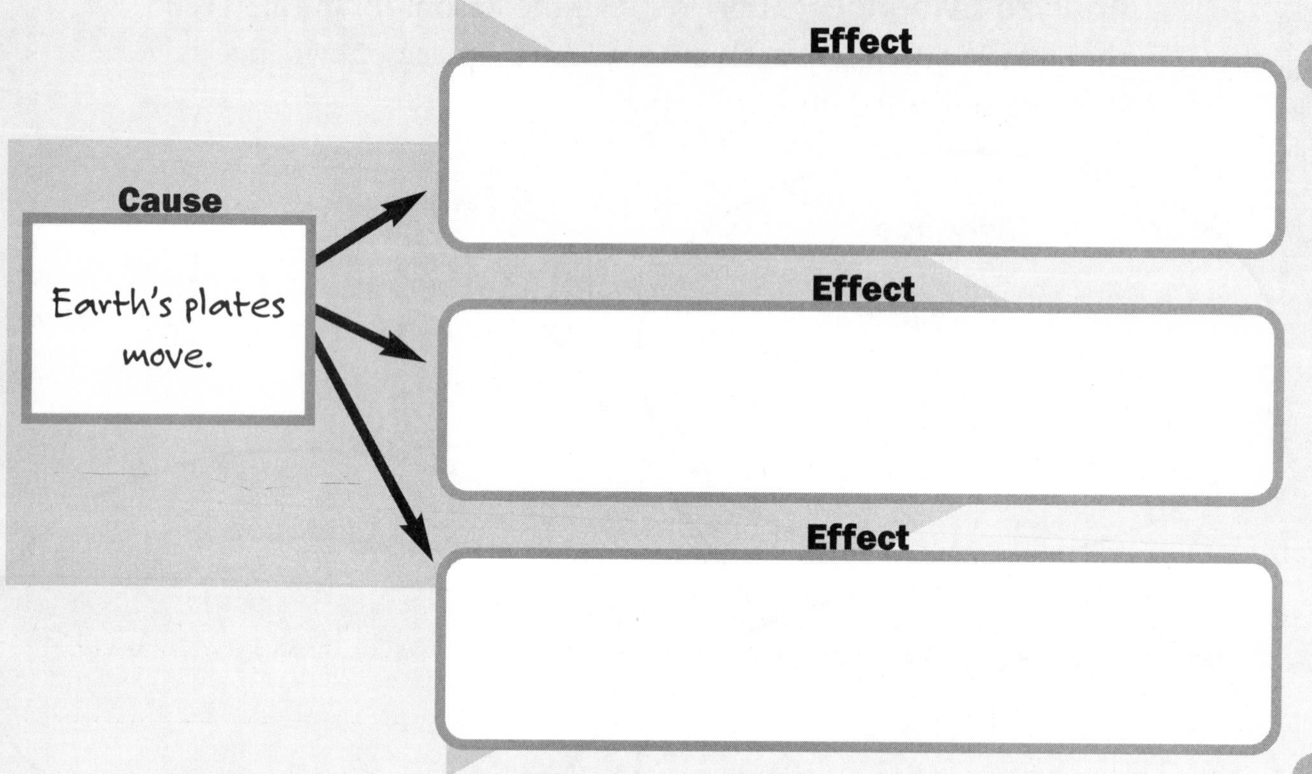

B. Key Facts Match each definition to the best word from the Word Bank. Write the letter of the word on the line.

1. _____ Big areas of salty water on Earth's top layer
2. _____ Large areas of land on Earth's crust
3. _____ Form when Earth's surface wrinkles
4. _____ Deep, low areas in the bottoms of oceans
5. _____ Happens when melted rock comes out of Earth
6. _____ Happens when the ground shakes

Word Bank

A. earthquake
B. volcano
C. oceans
D. mountains
E. trenches
F. continents

Name

FOR USE WITH PAGE 38

Showing What I Know

Summarizing In the box, draw a picture to show evidence that volcanoes let hot rock out of Earth. Label your picture. Then, on the lines, write a summary of the evidence shown in your picture.

My Summary of the Lesson

Name

All About Rocks

My Word List

A. Complete the Diagram As you read the lesson, complete this diagram with vocabulary words that describe parts of the rock cycle.

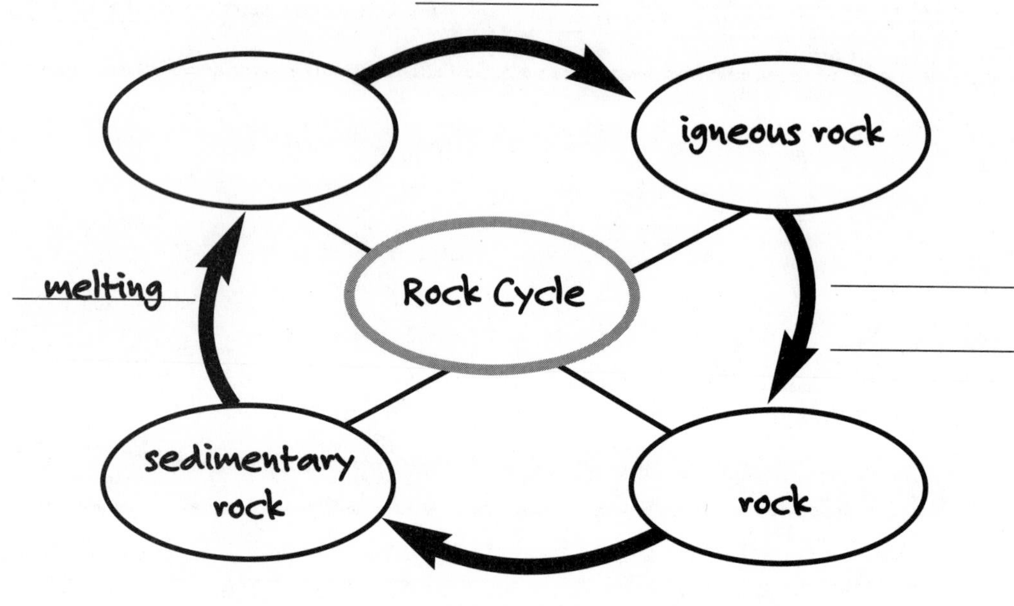

B. Writing Sentences Write 2–3 sentences explaining how the rock cycle works. Use at least 3 words from your Web.

Name

FOR USE WITH PAGE 43

Skill Building

Make Observations In the box, draw one of the kinds of rocks shown on page 41 of *ACCESS Science*. Include as many details as you can in your picture. Next, study your picture carefully. Then, write your observations about this kind of rock on the lines below.

Observations

1.

2.

3.

Name

My Study Notes

A. Study Skill: Outlining the Lesson Complete a study outline of this lesson. Use the headings on pages 44–49 of *ACCESS Science* to fill in the blanks.

1. Where Rock Forms
   a.
   b. Under the Ocean
2.
   a. Igneous Rock
   b.
   c.
3.

B. Picture Dictionary As you study the lesson, make a picture dictionary all about rocks. Draw pictures that will help you remember each term.

volcanoes	lava	seafloor spreading
sediment	layers	weathering

Name ______________________

FOR USE WITH PAGE 50

Showing What I Know

A. Interpreting Look at page 46 in *ACCESS Science* and study the rock the boy is holding. In the first column, write your observations about the rock. What kind of rock is it? Write your interpretation in the second column.

Topic:

Observations	Interpretations

B. Writing Sentences Use the details in your Observation Journal to write 2–3 sentences explaining your interpretation.

____

____

____

____

My Summary of the Lesson

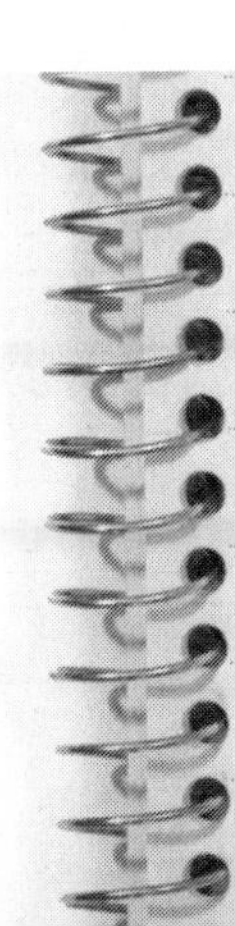

Name

The Changing Surface of Earth

My Word List

A. Definition Chart Find these words in the lesson. Write the definition and use the word in a sentence.

Word	Definition	Example Sentence
weathering		
erosion		
deposition		
expand		

B. Choosing Vocabulary Read each sentence below. Then underline the word that best completes the sentence.

1. (Deposition, Erosion) moves rock from one place to another.
2. Chemical (weathering, deposition) changes the chemicals inside rock.
3. Gravity affects (deposition, expand).
4. Ice can cause a crack in rock to (weather, expand).

Name ____________________

FOR USE WITH PAGE 55

Skill Building

A. Organize Data Mechanical weathering can be caused by water and by living things. As you study pages 56–57 in *ACCESS Science*, fill in this Venn Diagram with facts about these weathering causes. Put differences in the outside parts. Put similarities in the overlapping part.

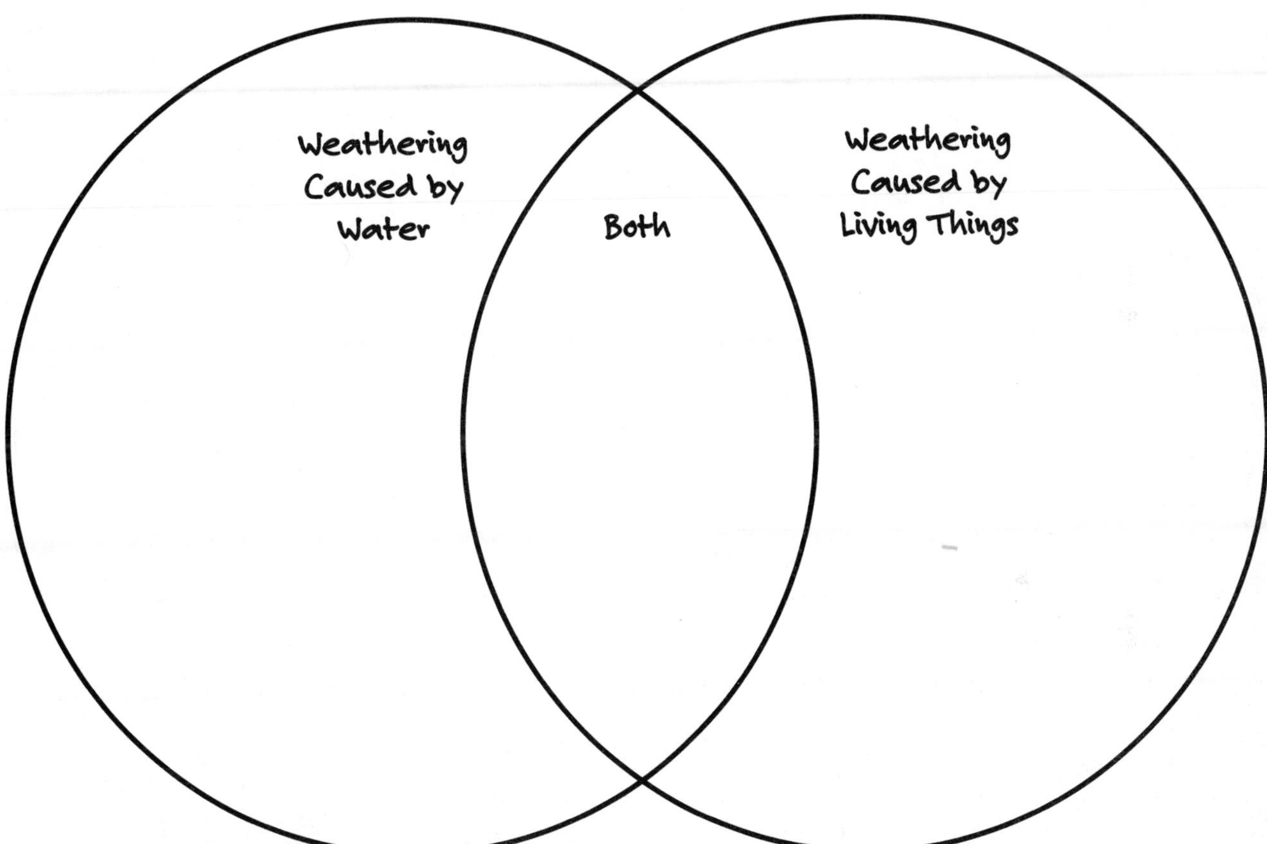

B. Writing Sentences Use the details from your Venn Diagram to write 2–3 sentences telling how the two kinds of mechanical weathering are alike and different.

____

____

____

____

Name

My Study Notes

A. Study Skill: Using Key Word or Topic Notes As you study the lesson, complete these Key Word or Topic Notes. Use information under the headings in your book for help.

Key Words or Topics	Notes
weathering	
erosion	
deposition	

B. Key Facts Use the Word Bank to complete these sentences.

1. ______________________ can cause rust.

2. Heat, wind, water, ice, and living things all cause ______________________.

3. A ______________ can be caused by just one rock slipping out of place.

4. Over thousands of years, ______________ can make U-shaped valleys in Earth's surface.

Word Bank

chemical weathering

landslide

mechanical weathering

glaciers

Name

FOR USE WITH PAGE 62

Showing What I Know

Comparing and Contrasting In the boxes below, draw a picture of a landslide and a picture of a flood. Below write two sentences that explain how landslides and floods are alike and different.

landslide	flood

My Summary of the Lesson

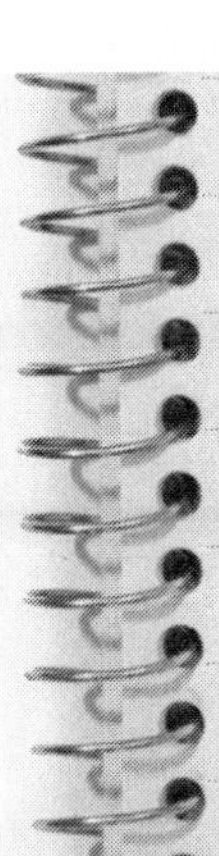

Name

Climate and Weather

My Word List

A. Web Write 2–3 sentences that tell how the 5 words below relate to each other.

B. Sentence Frame Use words from your Web to complete the sentences below. Then read the conversation aloud with a partner.

Maria: What do you think the weather will be like tomorrow?

Therese: I heard the ____________________ will go up to 107 degrees!

Maria: Wow! We have very hot ________________ here in the summer.

Therese: Sometimes it cools off a little after we get rain or other ____________________.

Name

FOR USE WITH PAGE 67

Skill Building

A. Look for Patterns Look at the temperatures and precipitation in this Weather Chart. Find the biggest change or changes in each row and circle where they are.

	MON	TUES	WED	THURS	FRI	SAT	SUN
High Temperature	86 °F	84 °F	71 °F	75 °F	77 °F	75 °F	76 °F
Low Temperature	65 °F	60 °F	53 °F	53 °F	58 °F	57 °F	57°F
Precipitation and Clouds	none	cloudy	cloudy	cloudy	rain	cloudy	rain

B. Writing Sentences Now use the details from your Weather Chart to write 2–3 sentences describing the changes and how they affect any pattern you see.

Name

My Study Notes

A. Study Skill: Using Sequence Notes Use information on pages 70–71 of *ACCESS Science* to complete these Sequence Notes about the water cycle. Remember to use signal words such as *next*, *then*, and *after*.

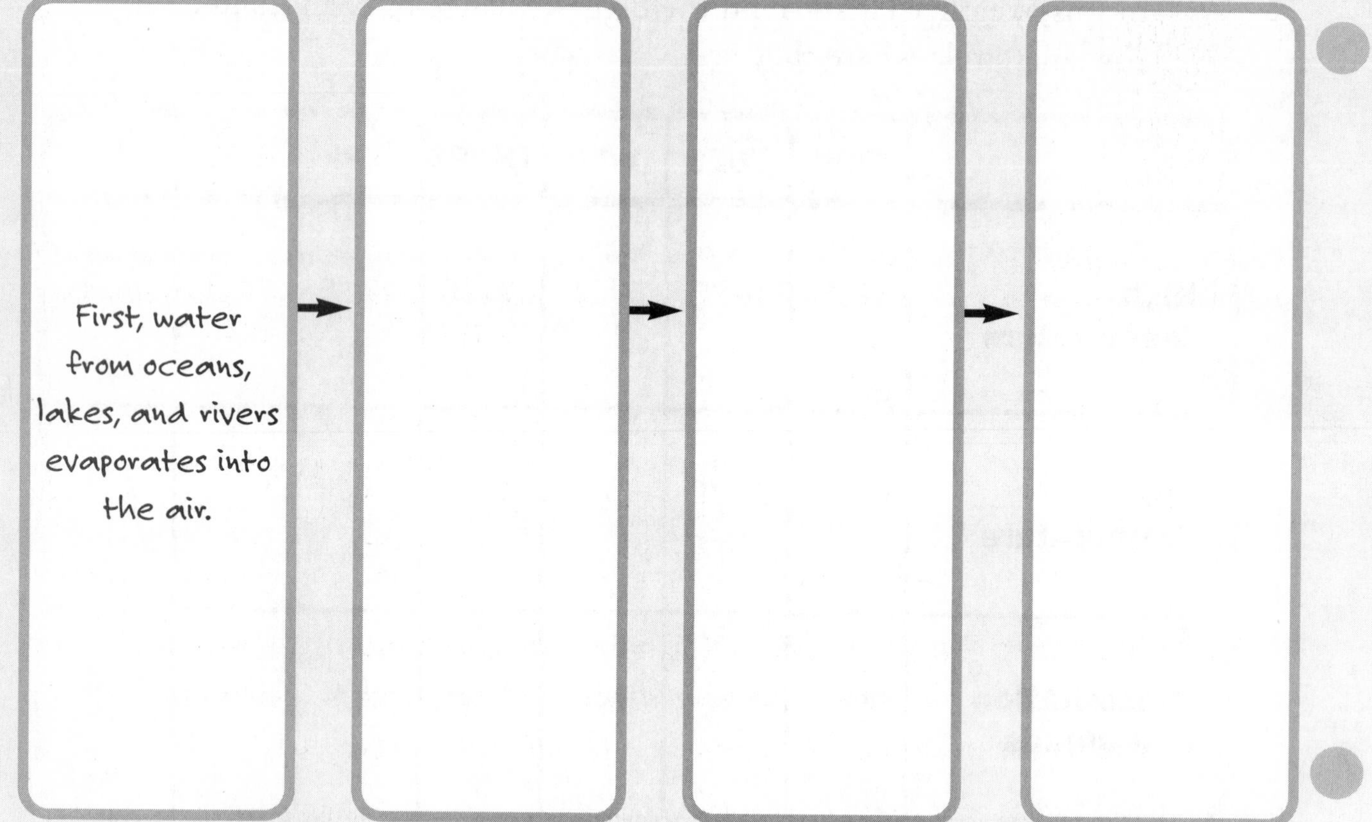

B. Key Facts Use the Word Bank to match each definition to the word it describes. Write the letter of the word on the line.

Word Bank

A. humidity
B. tropical
C. precipitation
D. temperate
E. solar energy
F. hurricane

1. _____ Warms the surface of Earth

2. _____ Can be in the form of fog, rain, snow, or sleet

3. _____ The climate zone that is near the equator

4. _____ A kind of storm that starts over the ocean

5. _____ Climate zones with both hot and cold seasons

6. _____ Measure of how much water is in the air

Name ______________________

FOR USE WITH PAGE 74

Showing What I Know

A. Predicting Draw 3 pictures that show the weather in your area for 3 days in a row. Then study your pictures. What do you think the weather will be like on day 4? Draw a picture in the last box to show your prediction.

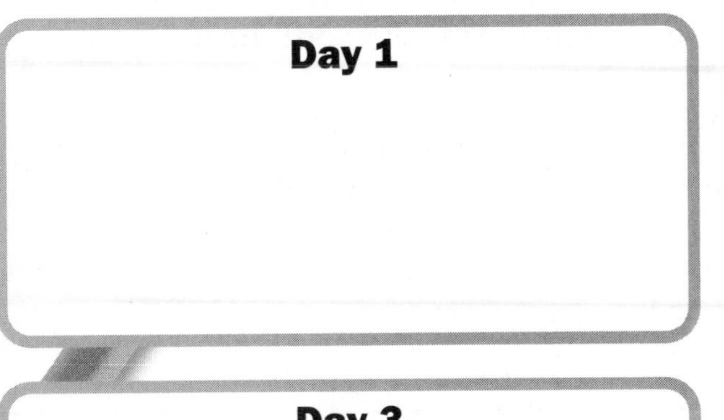

Day 1	**Day 2**
Day 3	**Day 4: My Prediction**

B. My Word Bank On the lines below, make a Word Bank that includes the words you need to describe your pictures. Then use the words to explain your weather prediction to a partner.

______________________ ______________________

______________________ ______________________

______________________ ______________________

______________________ ______________________

My Summary of the Lesson

Name

Earth, Sun, and Moon

My Word List

A. Definition Chart Find these words on pages 78–85 of *ACCESS Science*. Write the definition and use each word in a sentence.

Word	Definition	Example Sentence
rotates		
axis		
revolves		
orbits		
tilted		

B. Choosing Vocabulary In each sentence below, underline the word that best completes the sentence.

1. We have day and night because Earth (revolves, rotates) on its axis.
2. Earth's (axis, orbits) goes straight through the North Pole and the South Pole.
3. We have seasons because Earth (rotates, revolves) around the sun.
4. As the moon (orbits, rotates) Earth, we see different parts of the moon's surface.
5. It is summer in your town when your part of Earth is (axis, tilted) toward the sun.

Name ____________________

FOR USE WITH PAGE 79

Skill Building

A. Use a Model In the box below, draw a picture to show the positions of Earth and the sun when it is 12:00 noon in your town. Use the pictures and information on pages 80–81 of *ACCESS Science* for help.

B. Writing Sentences Now use the details from your picture to write 1–3 sentences explaining what your model shows.

Name

My Study Notes

A. Study Skill: Outlining the Lesson Complete a study outline of this lesson. Use the headings in *ACCESS Science* to fill in the blanks.

1. Day and Night
   a. Rotation
   b.
   c.
2. Seasons
   a.
   b. Spring and Fall
3.
   a. Moon and Sun
   b.
4. Eclipses
   a.
   b.

B. Key Facts Use the Word Bank to complete these sentences.

1. Summer, winter, spring, and fall are the 4 ________________.
2. Tides are caused mostly by the gravity of the ________________.
3. The terms *waxing crescent* and *waning gibbous* refer to two of the moon's ________________.
4. In a ________________, the moon partly blocks the sun's light on Earth.
5. When Earth makes a shadow on the moon, the event is called a ________________.

Word Bank

solar eclipse
phases
lunar eclipse
seasons
moon

Name

FOR USE WITH PAGE 86

Showing What I Know

Describing In the space below, draw a model of a lunar eclipse. Include the positions of the sun, moon, and Earth in your picture. Then on the lines, write sentences to describe your model and tell what it shows.

My Summary of the Lesson

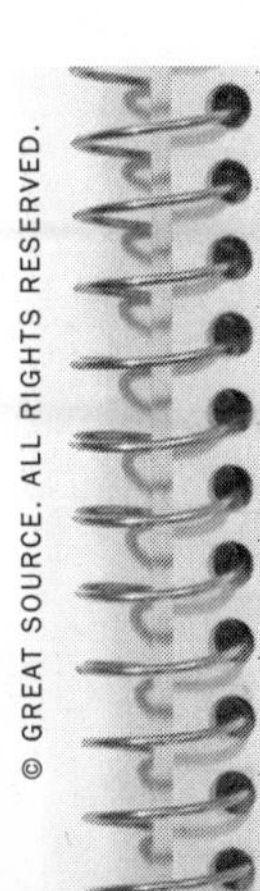

Name

Natural Resources

My Word List

A. What Is It? Below, write a sentence that tells what each word means and how it relates to the world around you.

resource ______________________________

renewable ______________________________

renew ______________________________

nonrenewable ______________________________

conserving ______________________________

B. Sentence Frame Use the words above to complete the paragraph below.

A natural ____________ is something people use to make energy, grow food, or build things. The wind and the sun are ____________ resources. Coal and oil are ____________ resources, which means we may run out of them. ____________ nonrenewable resources will help them last longer. Recycling is one way to do this. Each time that you recycle a drink can you ____________ a resource!

Name

FOR USE WITH PAGE 91

Skill Building

A. Use Math to Organize Data Conduct a survey to find out how the people in your class dry their hair after washing it. What percentage of your class uses energy from electricity (a hair dryer) and what percentage uses energy from wind and air? Fill in and label the pie chart below to show your data. Use the steps on page 91 of *ACCESS Science* to complete your chart.

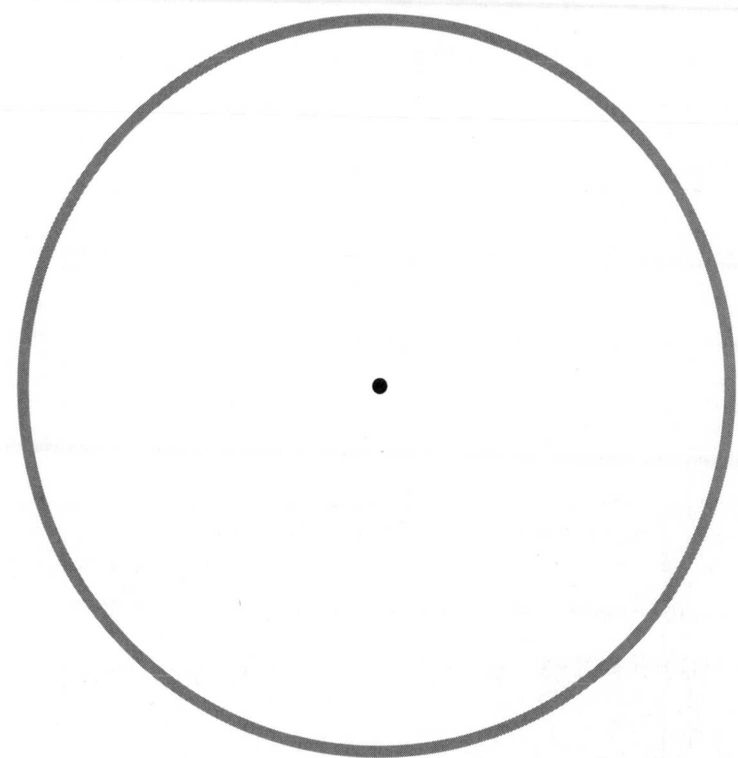

B. My Word Bank Write the words and phrases you need to explain the data in your pie chart. Then explain your chart to a partner.

Name

My Study Notes

A. Study Skill: Using a Main Idea Organizer

As you study the lesson, use pages 92–97 of *ACCESS Science* to complete this Main Idea Organizer about natural resources. Write notes about each detail in the boxes. Then write a sentence to tell your conclusion.

Main Idea: People use natural resources to help make life better.

Detail	Detail	Detail
Renewable Resources	Nonrenewable Resources	Conserving Resources

My Conclusion:

B. Key Facts

Use the Word Bank to match each sentence with the resource it describes. Write the letter of the resource on the line.

1. ____ This is all the renewable resources that come from living things.

2. ____ Oil and coal are two examples of these resources.

3. ____ This kind of energy comes from a change to the atoms in uranium.

4. ____ This type of fossil fuel is invisible.

5. ____ This renewable resource can only be used where there is heat inside Earth.

6. ____ Water wheels can help create this renewable resource.

Word Bank

A. nuclear energy
B. fossil fuels
C. biomass
D. hydroelectric power
E. geothermal energy
F. natural gas

Name ______________________________

FOR USE WITH PAGE 98

Showing What I Know

Summarizing This pie chart shows the energy resources for Powertown. First, fill in the key. Write the percentage of each energy resource on its line in the key. Then, write one or two sentences to summarize how much of Powertown's energy comes from renewable and nonrenewable resources.

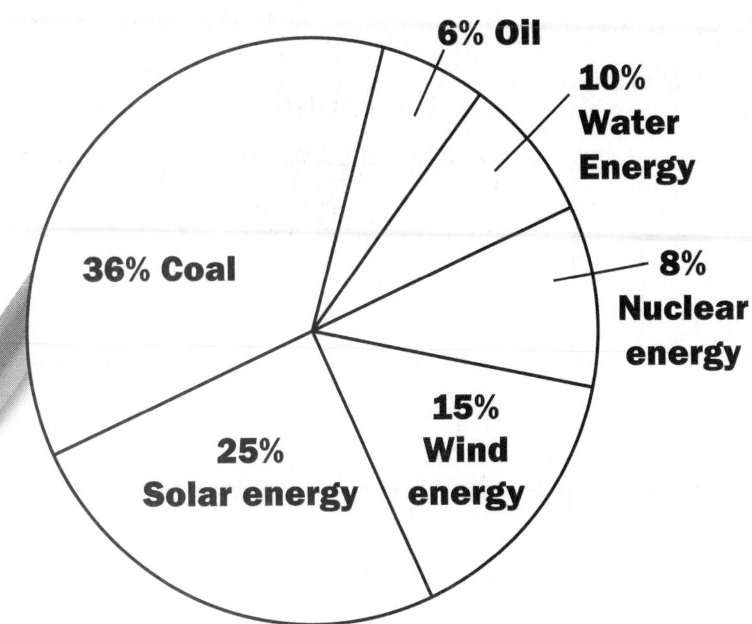

Energy Resources for Powertown

Key	
Coal	____%
Solar energy	____%
Wind energy	____%
Water energy	____%
Nuclear energy	____%
Oil	____%

My Data Summary

____

____

____

____

____

My Summary of the Lesson

____

____

____

____

____

____

Name

How People Affect Earth

My Word List

A. Word Pictures Use the spaces below to draw the global environment and an example of a habitat.

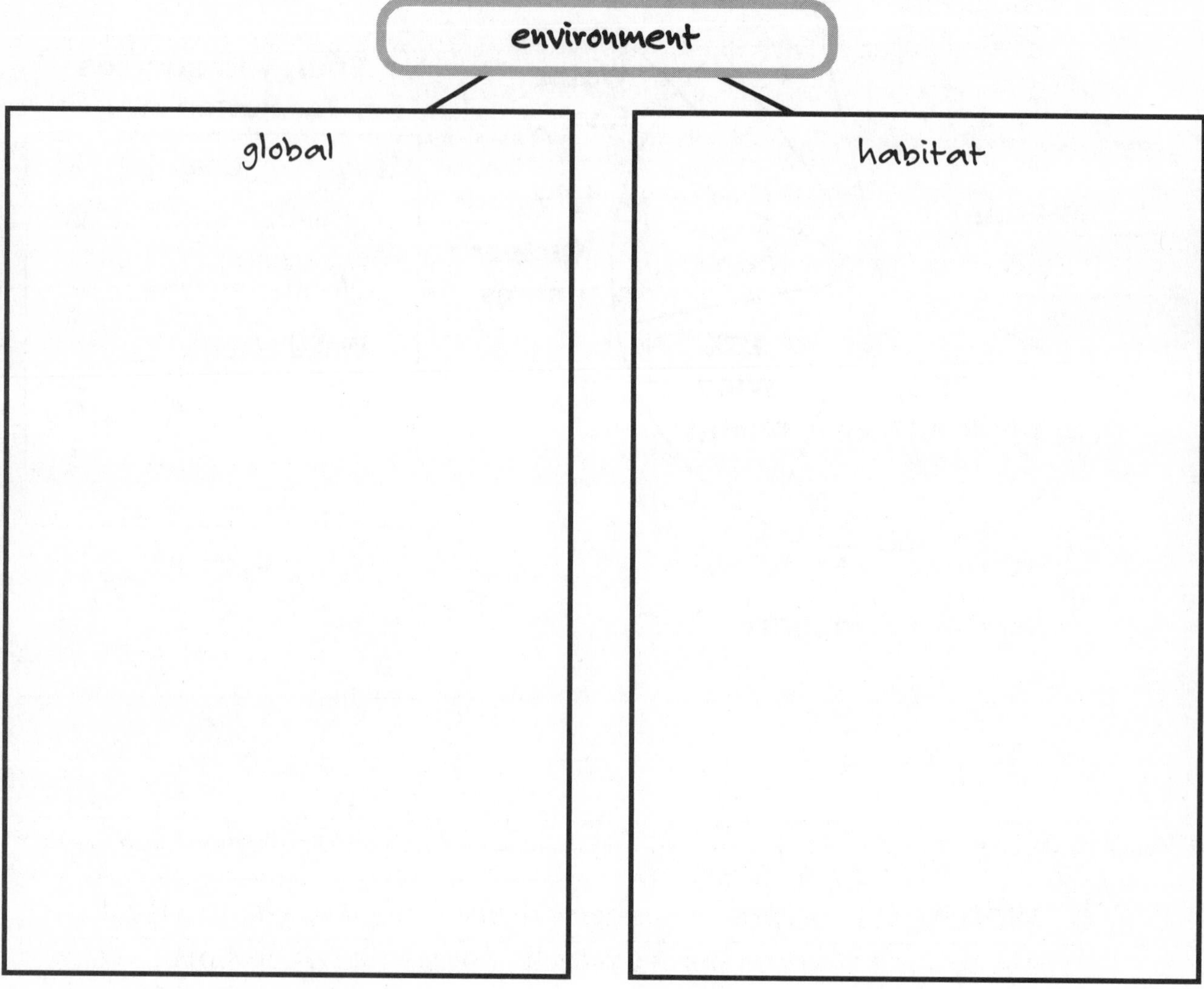

B. Writing Sentences Write 2–3 sentences to explain each of your drawings.

Name

FOR USE WITH PAGE 103

Skill Building

A. Infer from Evidence Fill in the chart below to show two examples of recycling in your neighborhood. Think about where your family and neighbors put different kinds of trash. Write observations in the first column. Then use what you already know, plus your observations, to write your inference in the second column.

Topic: Recycling in my neighborhood	
Evidence (observations)	**Inference**

B. Writing Sentences Use the evidence from your chart to think about ways you can improve recycling in your neighborhood. Write 2–3 sentences to tell your suggestions.

Name ____________________

My Study Notes

A. Study Skill: Using Key Word or Topic Notes Complete the Key Word or Topic Notes below for this lesson. Use the information under the headings in *ACCESS Science*.

Key Words or Topics	Notes
Where people live	
Pollution	
Global climate change	
Helping earth	

B. Key Facts Use the Word Bank to complete these sentences.

Word Bank
- greenhouse gases
- population
- pollution
- conserve

1. Many cities have a ________________ of more than a million people.
2. Most air ________________ is caused by cars and other motor vehicles.
3. ________________ stop some of Earth's heat from leaving the atmosphere.
4. You can ________________ water by turning it off while you brush your teeth.

Name

FOR USE WITH PAGE 110

Showing What I Know

Explaining Fill in this Web to make an inference about how pollution affects your habitat. Think about things people do that are harmful to the land, water, and air. Write evidence in the 3 circles. Then write your inference.

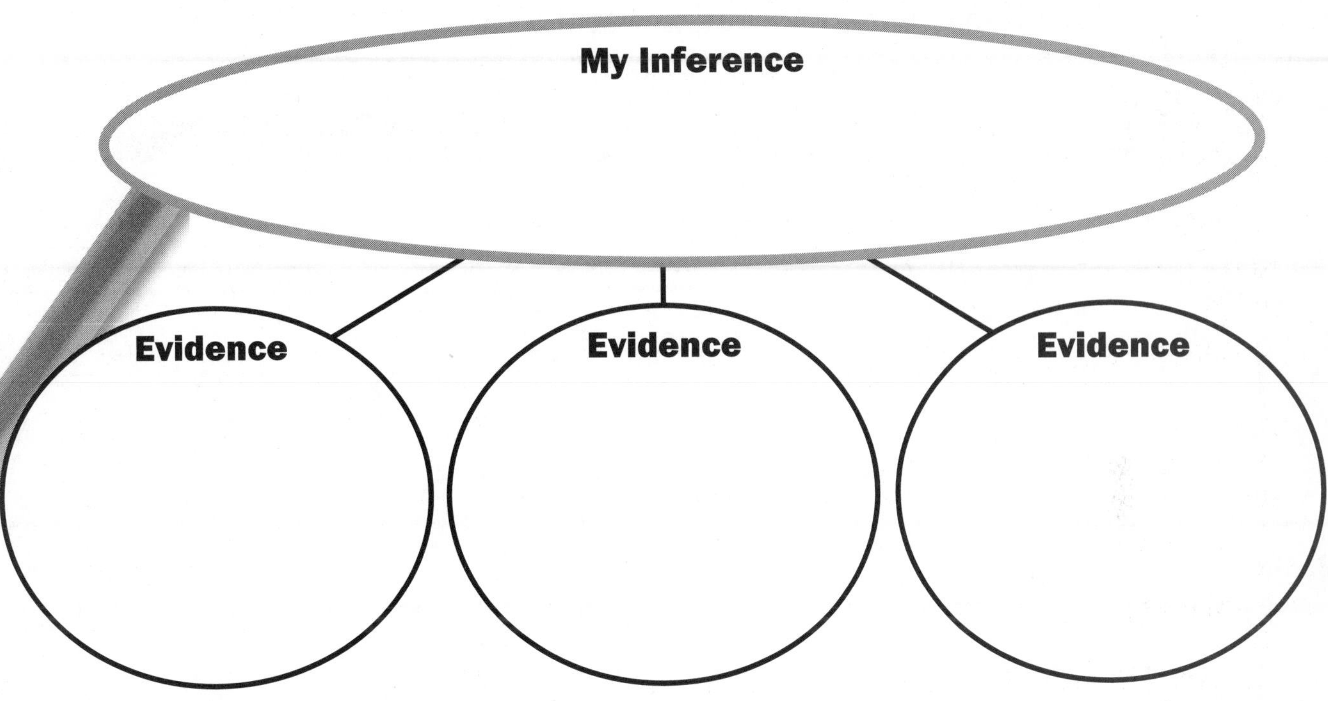

Write 3–4 sentences that state your inference and explain it. Tell how the evidence supports your conclusion.

My Summary of the Lesson

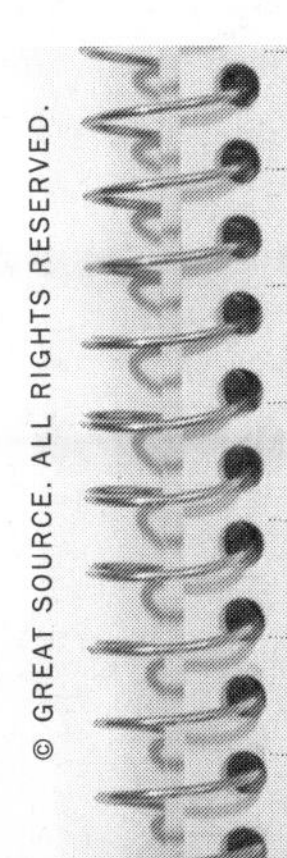

Name

Exploring Ecology

My Word List

A. Definition Chart Find these words in the lesson. Then write the definition and use the word in a sentence.

Word	Definition	Example Sentence
ecology		
interact		
ecosystem		
species		
community		

B. Choosing Vocabulary Underline the word that best completes each sentence below.

1. The science of living things and their environments is called (ecology, ecosystem).
2. Plants and animals (interact, community) with one another in an ecosystem.
3. A (community, ecology) is made up of different species living in one environment.
4. Cactus plants and snakes are parts of a desert (ecosystem, species).
5. Every plant and animal is a member of a (species, ecology).

Name ______________________________

FOR USE WITH PAGE 115

Skill Building

A. Think About Systems Use the information on page 116 of *ACCESS Science* to complete this Web showing the parts of a desert ecosystem. Include both living and nonliving things.

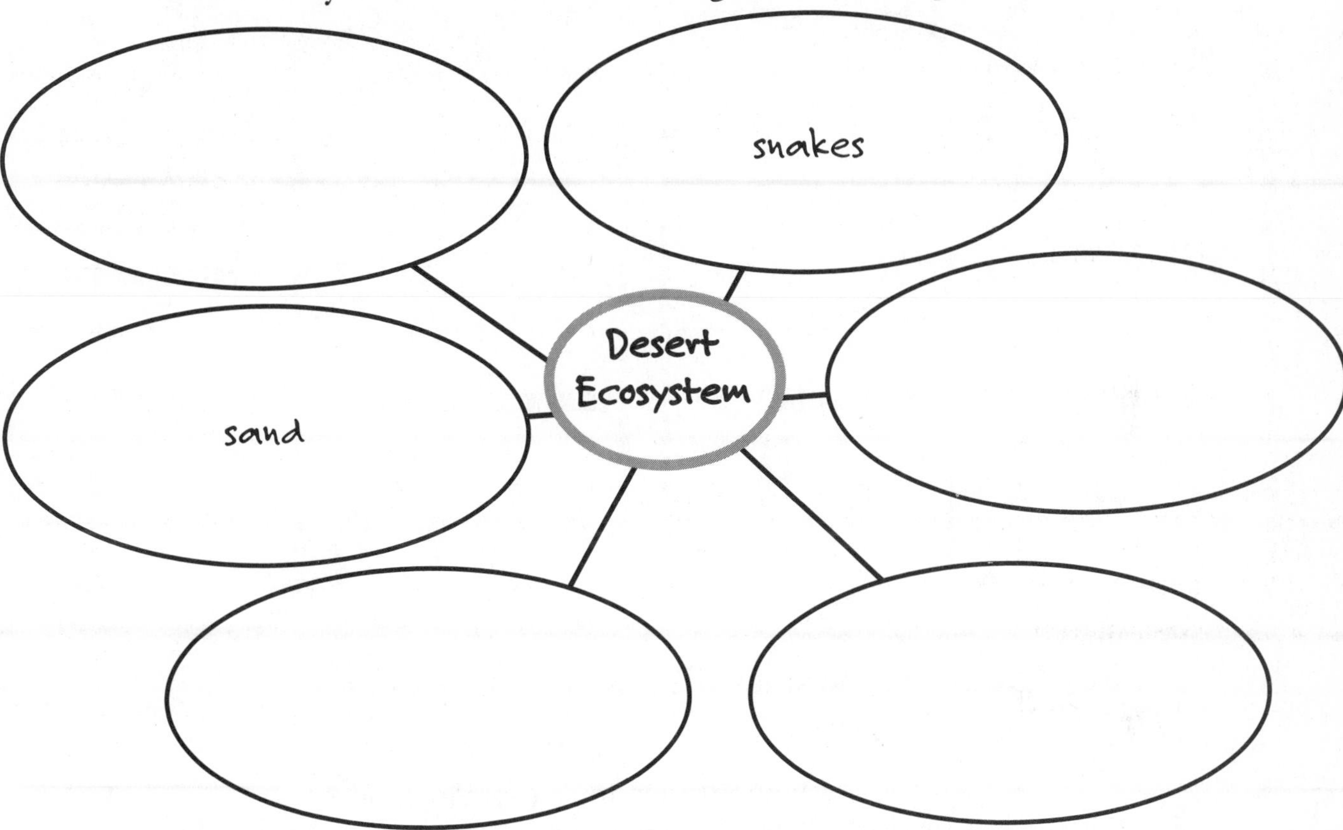

B. Writing Sentences Use the words from your Web to write 2–3 sentences that tell how the parts of a desert ecosystem work together.

____

____

____

____

____

____

____

Name

My Study Notes

A. Study Skill: Using Sequence Notes Use the information on page 120 of *ACCESS Science* to complete the Sequence Notes below. Write the definition of each group and give an example.

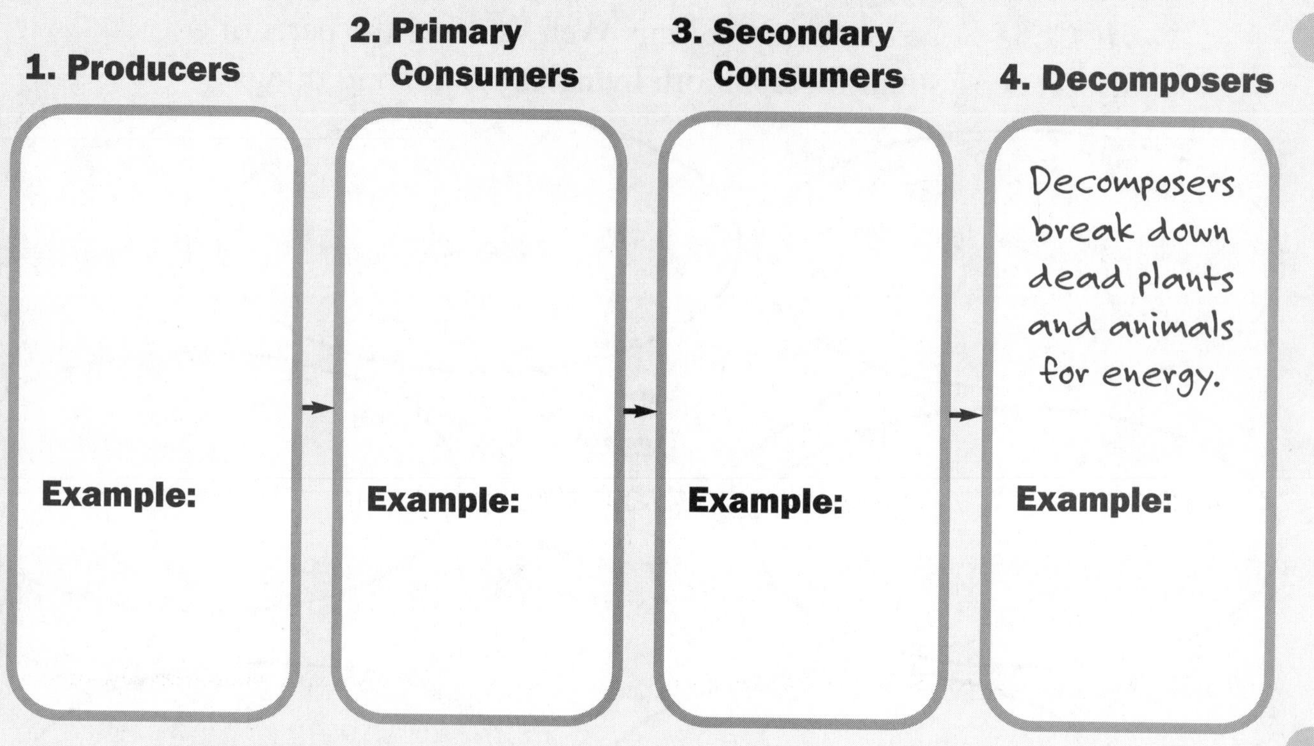

B. Key Facts As you study the lesson, use the Word Bank to complete these sentences.

1. The ______________ of living things in one environment make up a community.
2. Sunlight provides the ______________ that makes life in an ecosystem possible.
3. ______________ give plants and animals the energy they need to live and grow.
4. During the carbon ______________, animals eat carbon in plants and release carbon dioxide.
5. Energy moves from producer plants to consumer animals in a ______________.

Word Bank
- nutrients
- cycle
- populations
- food chain
- energy

Name

FOR USE WITH PAGE 122

Showing What I Know

Explaining In the box, draw a picture of the ecosystem in which you live. Include both living and nonliving things. Add labels for the parts of the ecosystem.

Use your labels in 3–4 sentences to explain how parts of your ecosystem interact.

My Summary of the Lesson

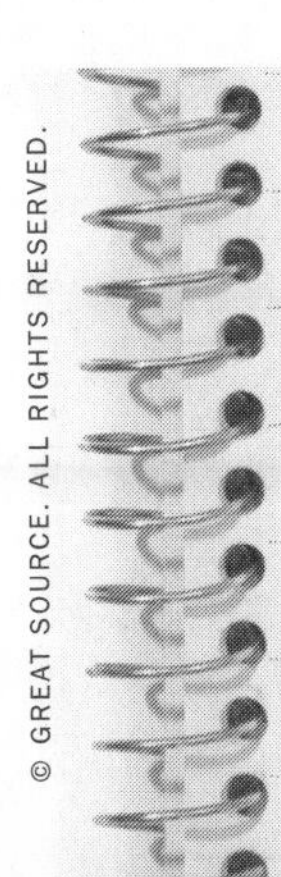

Name ______________________

FOR USE WITH PAGES 126–133

Life's Diversity

My Word List

A. Definition Chart Find these words in the lesson. Write the definition and use each word in a sentence. Use the *ACCESS Science* glossary for help.

Word	Definition	Example Sentence
characteristics		
diversity		
classify		
category		

B. Sentence Frame Complete each sentence below using words from the chart above.

1. When I ________________ a living thing, I start by making observations.
2. Every ________________ of life has different characteristics.
3. ________________ include colors and shapes I can observe.
4. Scientists classify living things because of life's great ________________.

Name

FOR USE WITH PAGE 127

Skill Building

A. Make Observations Fill in the Classification Organizer to record characteristics of a tree you can observe or imagine. Observe or imagine the tree, and then fill in the Observation column.

Characteristic	Observation
Where it lives	
Its color(s)	
Unicellular or multicellular?	
How it gets energy	

B. Use Signal Words Use the details from your organizer to write 3 sentences about why the tree is a member of the plant kingdom. Remember to use signal words, such as *kinds*, *characteristics*, *group*, *category*, and *includes*.

Name ____________________

My Study Notes

A. Study Skill: Using Classification Notes Complete these Classification Notes for the lesson. Use headings and details from *ACCESS Science* to fill in the empty parts.

Kingdom	Cell Type and Number	Other Details
archaebacteria	prokaryote	
eubacteria		3 shapes:
protists	eukaryote	
		decomposers
plants		producers
	eukaryote	

B. Key Facts Use the Word Bank to complete these sentences.

1. My ______________ is *Homo sapiens.*
2. A eukaryotic cell has a ______________, but a prokaryotic cell does not.
3. When cells do different jobs, they are ______________.
4. Living things come in many ______________.
5. I can observe different ______________ when I look at a living thing.

Word Bank

- nucleus
- characteristics
- specialized
- varieties
- scientific name

Name

FOR USE WITH PAGE 134

Showing What I Know

Classifying Draw a picture of a living thing you have observed this week. Write the words you need to classify this organism in the Word Bank below. Then tell a partner the characteristics you used to classify the living thing.

My Word Bank

My Summary of the Lesson

Name

Cell Structure

My Word List

A. Definition Web Write definitions in the ovals to complete the Definition Web below.

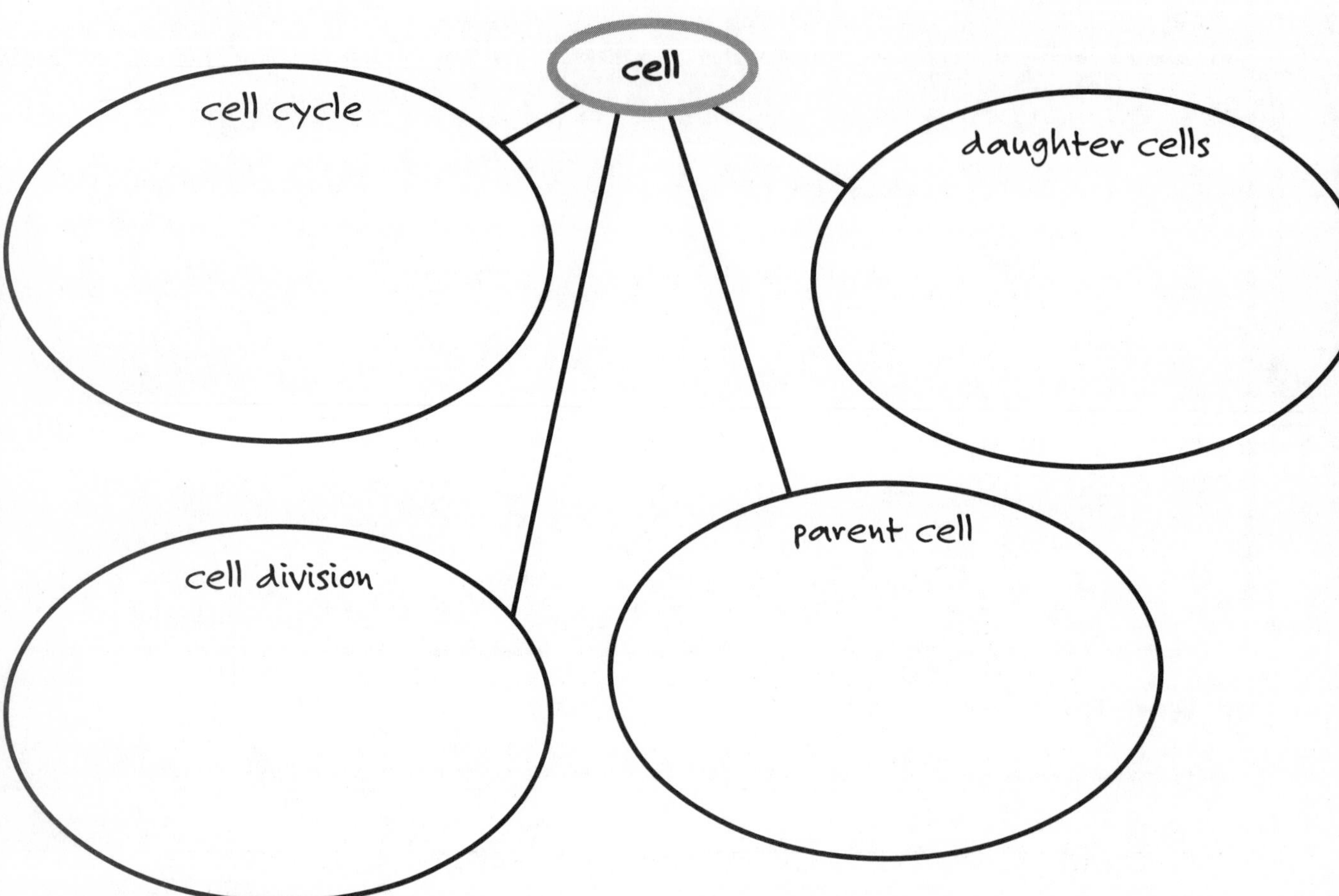

B. Writing Sentences Now write 3–4 sentences describing the steps in the cell cycle. Use words from your Definition Web.

Name

FOR USE WITH PAGE 139

Skill Building

A. Visualize Draw a picture in the box to help you visualize an animal cell. Use the diagrams on pages 137 and 141 of *ACCESS Science* to help you.

B. My Word Bank Now write words to describe your picture. Include names for the different parts of the animal cell. Then label your picture.

Name

My Study Notes

A. Study Skill: Using a Web Use the information on pages 140–141 of *ACCESS Science* to complete this Web. Write the job of each cell part in the ovals.

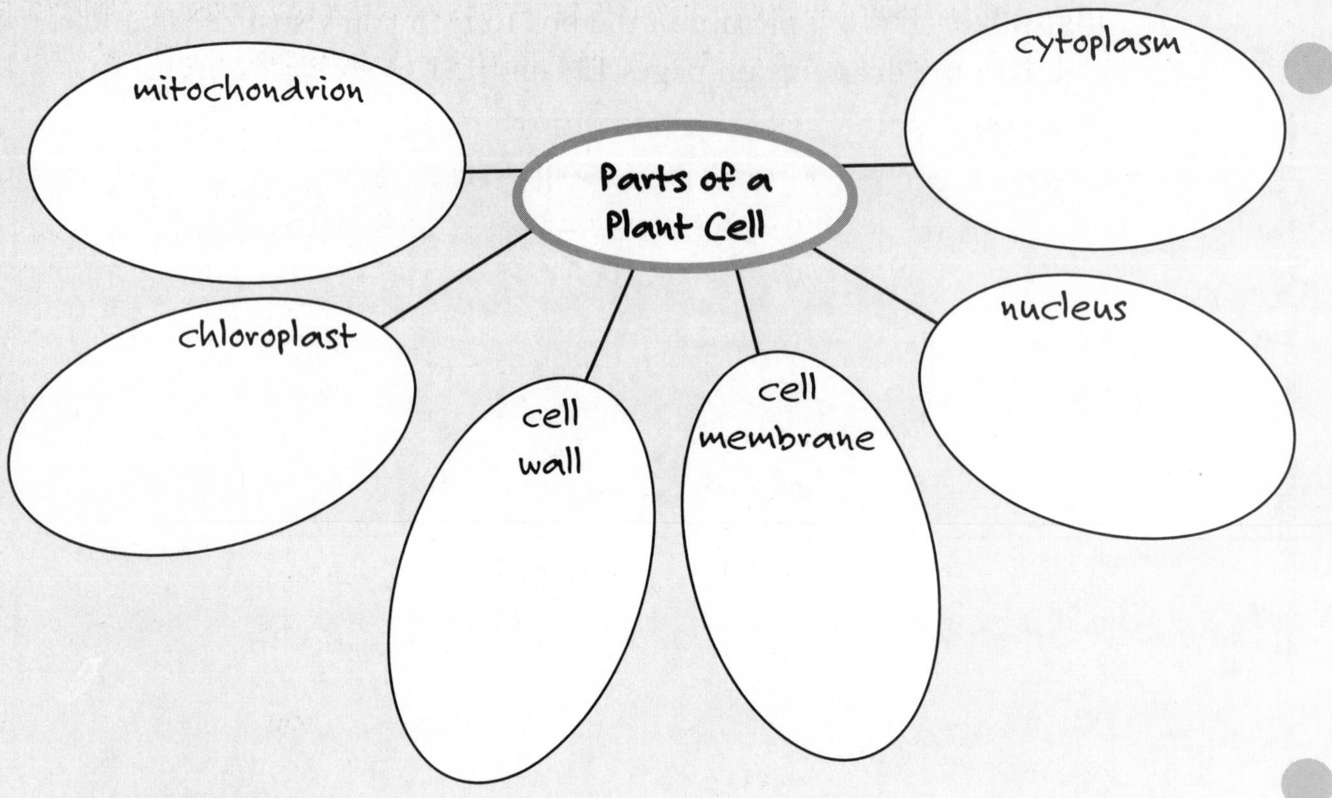

B. Key Facts After you read the lesson, match each definition with the word it describes. Write the letter of the word on the line.

Word Bank

A. organelles
B. photosynthesis
C. eukaryotic
D. mitosis
E. chromosomes
F. cell division
G. cancer

1. _____ A cell that has a nucleus

2. _____ Parts that do special jobs in eukaryotic cells

3. _____ A disease caused by out-of-control cell division

4. _____ Structures that hold all the information a cell needs to pass on when it divides

5. _____ How plants use sunlight to make food

6. _____ The set of stages in the division of a cell's nucleus

7. _____ How cells copy themselves

Name ____________________

FOR USE WITH PAGE 146

Showing What I Know

A. Comparing and Contrasting Use the Venn Diagram to compare and contrast animal cells and plant cells.

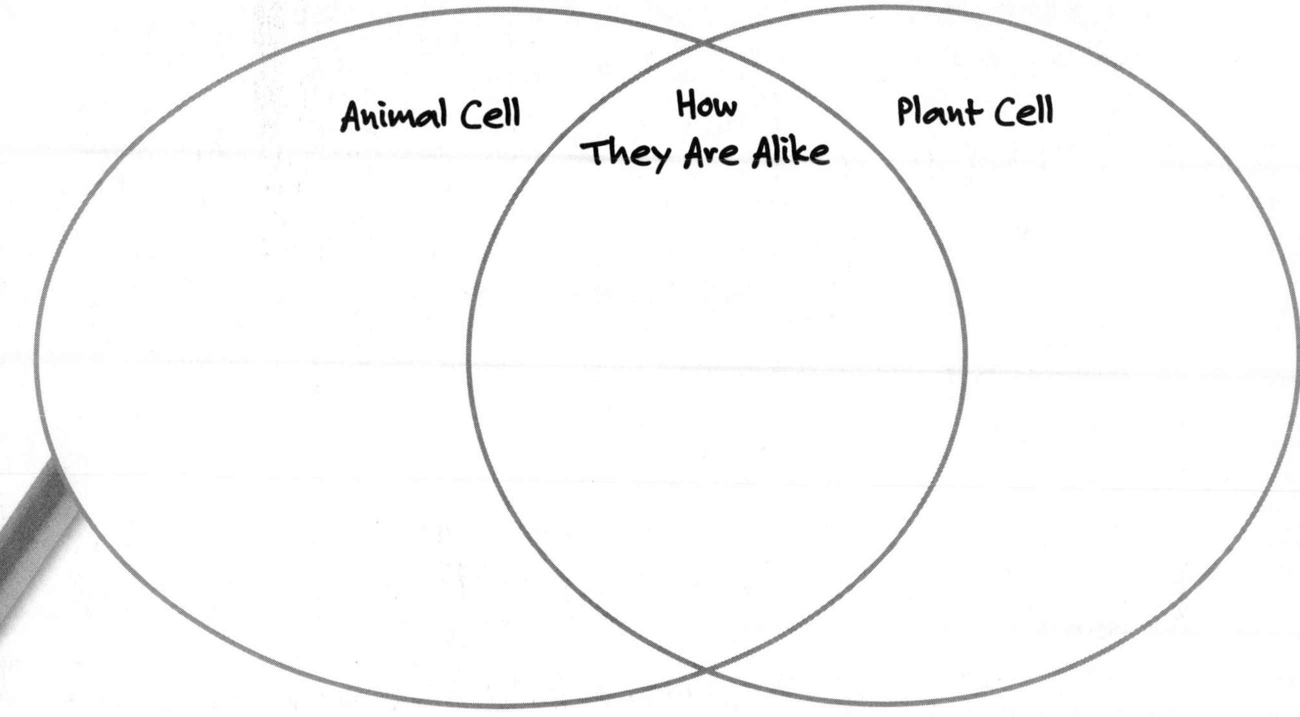

B. Writing Sentences Write 3–4 sentences telling how animal cells and plant cells are alike and different. Use the details in your Venn Diagram.

____

____

____

____

My Summary of the Lesson

Name

Cells to Organisms

My Word List

A. What Is It? Write a sentence to explain each word below.

structure
____
____
What is it?

function
____
____
What is it?

tissues
____
____
What are they?

organs
____
____
What are they?

organ systems
____
____
What are they?

B. Completing a Paragraph Use the words above to complete the paragraph below.

From cells to organ systems, each part of your body is a _______________. Each of these has a different job, or _______________. The smallest part of your body is a cell. Cells work together in _______________. Different tissues make up _______________. Different organs work together in _______________.

Name ______________________

FOR USE WITH PAGE 151

Skill Building

A. Organize Data Use information from page 153 of *ACCESS Science* to fill in this Size Organizer about muscles. Put the parts in order from smallest to largest.

muscular system

skeletal muscle fiber

skeletal muscle bundle

leg muscle

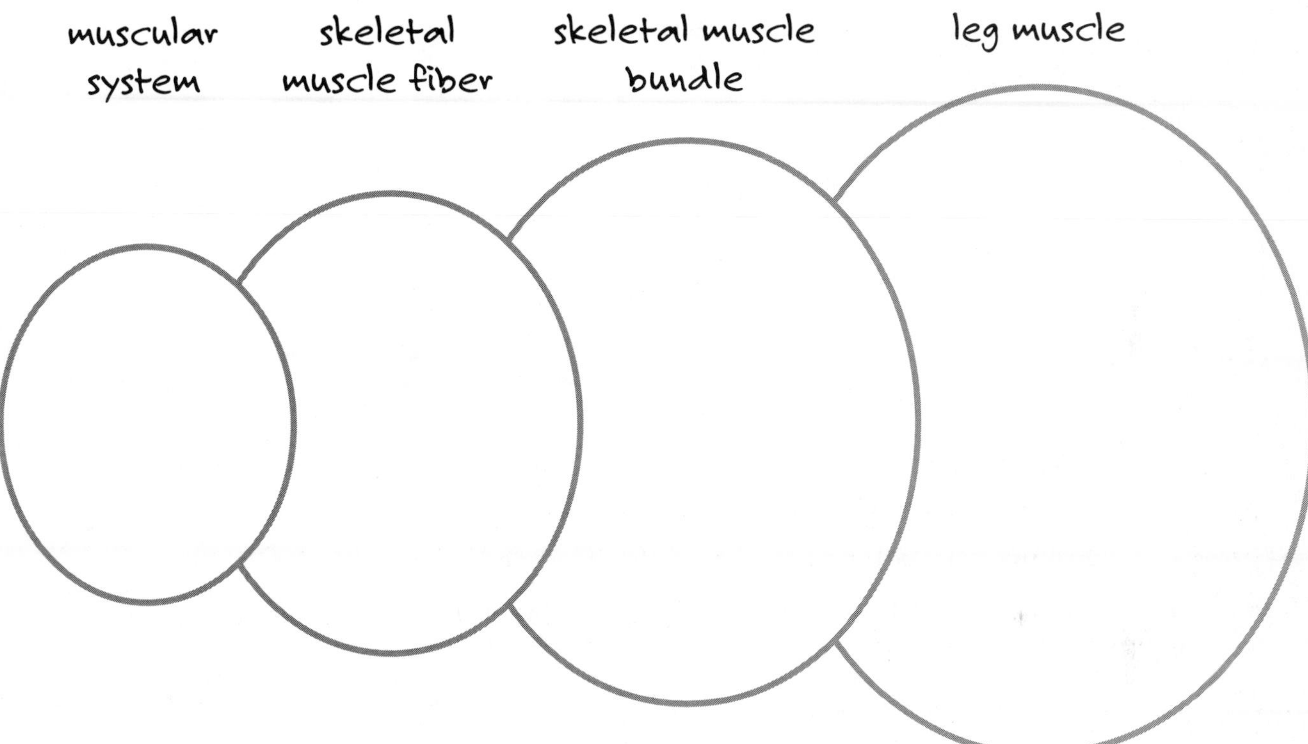

B. Writing Sentences Use the details from your organizer to write 2–3 sentences telling how these parts of the muscular system are related.

____

____

____

____

____

____

____

Name

My Study Notes

A. Study Skill: Using a Two-column Chart Complete a Two-column Chart for this lesson. Write body structures in the left column. Write their functions in the right column. Include examples of cells, tissues, organs, and organ systems.

Structure	Function
• red blood cells	• carry oxygen around the body

B. Picture Dictionary As you read the lesson, make a picture dictionary of parts of the human body. For each term, draw a picture that helps you remember the structure and its function. You can use pictures in *ACCESS Science* for help.

muscle	heart	tissues
blood vessels	circulatory system	digestive system

Name

FOR USE WITH PAGE 158

Showing What I Know

Describing Think of a structure in your body that you learned about in this lesson. Or think of a structure that is part of your everyday life, such as a bicycle or a house. Fill in the Size Organizer to show the parts of the structure from smallest to largest. Write the name of your structure in the bottom section of the organizer.

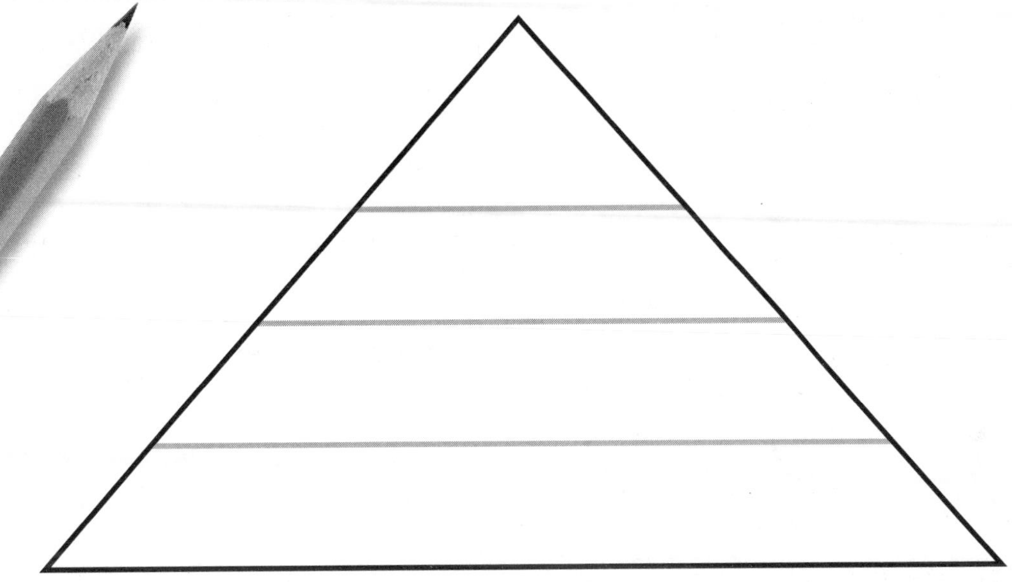

Write 3–4 sentences describing how the parts of your structure work together. Use the details from your Size Organizer.

My Summary of the Lesson

Name

Energy and Nutrients

My Word List

A. Word Web Complete the Word Web below with vocabulary words from the lesson. In the ovals, write things that give your body energy.

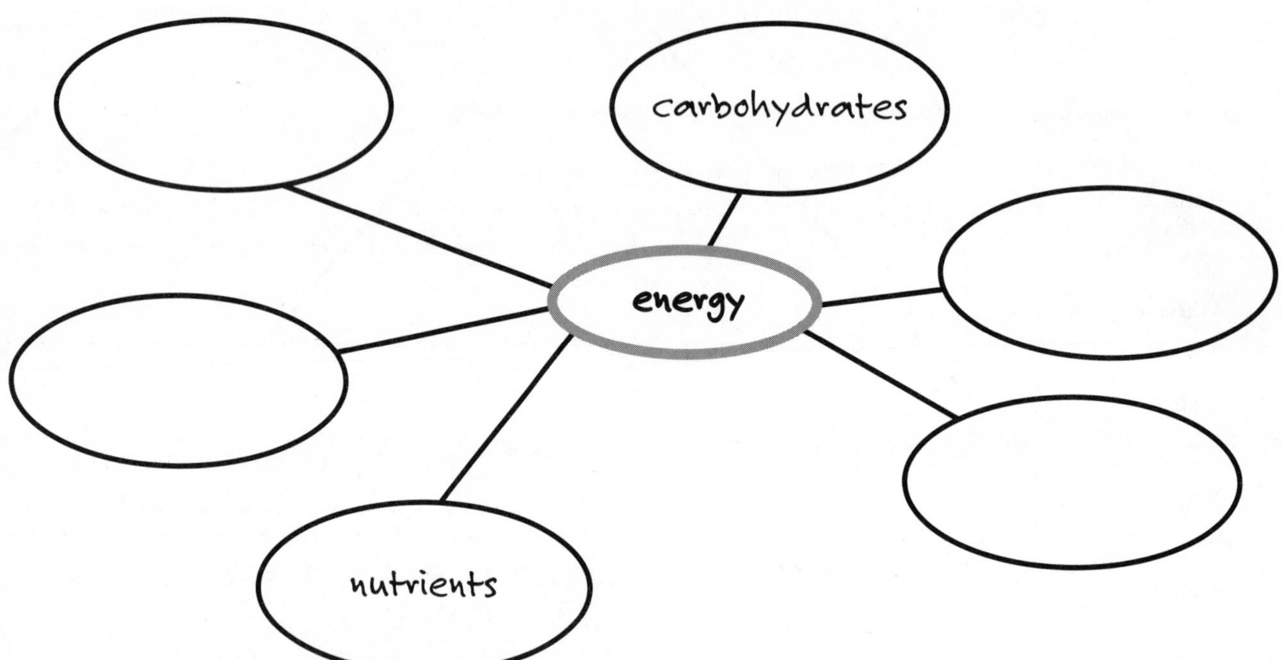

B. Drawing and Writing In the space below, draw a picture of a food you think gives your body energy. Then on the lines write 3–4 sentences about your picture. Use at least 3 words from your Word Web.

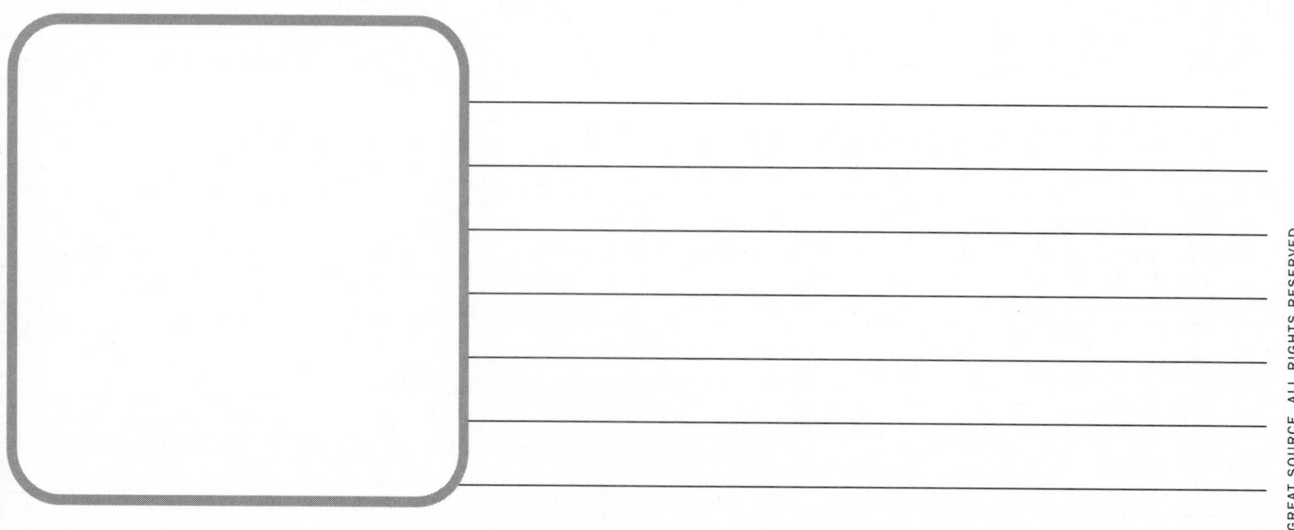

Name ____________________

FOR USE WITH PAGE 163

Skill Building

A. Use Math Complete this chart to show how many daily Calories should come from each nutrient for teen girls and boys. Multiply the total recommended Calories by the percent for each nutrient. For example, 2,200 × 30% = 2,200 × 0.30 = 660 daily Calories from fat for a teen girl.

Nutrient	Percent of Daily Calories Needed	Recommended Calories: Teen Girl	Recommended Calories: Teen Boy
Carbohydrates	60		
Fats	30	660	
Proteins	10		
Total	100	2,200	2,800

B. Writing Sentences Use the details from your chart to write 2–3 sentences about your own daily Calorie needs. Which nutrient should you eat to get most of your Calories?

____

____

____

____

____

____

____

____

____

Name ______________________________

My Study Notes

A. Study Skill: Using Key Word or Topic Notes Use the information under the red headings in *ACCESS Science* to complete the Key Word or Topic Notes below. Write notes about each topic in the second column.

Key Words or Topics	Notes
Turning Energy into Food	
How to Turn Food into Energy	
What Are Nutrients?	

B. Key Facts As you read the lesson, use the Word Bank to match each sentence with the word it describes. Write the letter of the word on the line.

Word Bank

A. calcium

B. cellular respiration

C. minerals

D. vitamins

1. ______ Milk and cheese contain this bone-building mineral.

2. ______ In this process, cells break down food to make energy.

3. ______ These nutrients help cells do their jobs. They contain carbon.

4. ______ These nutrients help support your body's structures.

Name ______________________

FOR USE WITH PAGE 170

Showing What I Know

A. Interpreting Study these food labels for different snacks. On each label, find and circle the grams and the percent Daily Value of total fat. Then do the same for total carbohydrate, using boxes instead of circles. Which snack do you think is better for your body?

Nutrition Facts
Serving Size 3 cookies (26 g)
Servings Per Container 6
Amount Per Serving

Calories 100	Calories from Fat 20
	% Daily Value
Total Fat 2 g	3%
Saturated Fat 0 g	
Cholesterol 0 mg	0%
Sodium 170 mg	7%
Total Carbohydrate 20 g	7%
Dietary Fiber Less than 1 g	3%
Sugars 9 g	
Protein 1 g	

Nutrition Facts
Serving Size 18 puffs (28 g)
Servings Per Container 4.5
Amount Per Serving

Calories 130	Calories from Fat 60
	% Daily Value
Total Fat 6 g	10%
Saturated Fat 1 g	
Cholesterol 0 mg	0%
Sodium 150 mg	5%
Total Carbohydrate 17 g	6%
Dietary Fiber 2 g	8%
Sugars 1 g	
Protein 2 g	

B. Writing Sentences Write 3–4 sentences explaining your snack choice.

____

____

____

____

____

My Summary of the Lesson

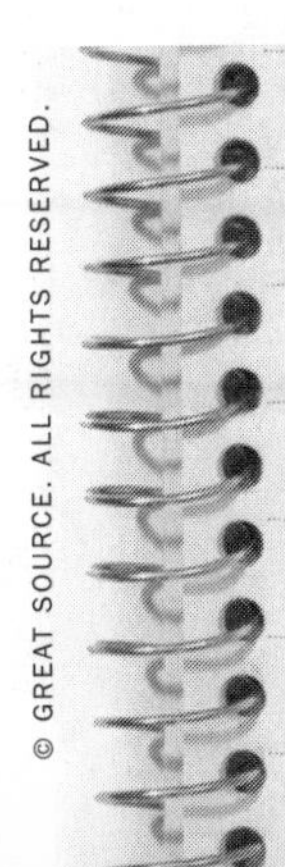

Name

Responding to the Environment

My Word List

A. Definition Chart Find these words in the lesson. Write the definition and use each word in a sentence.

Word	Definition	Example Sentence
equilibrium		
senses		
stimulus		
response		
reflexes		

B. Choosing Vocabulary Read each sentence below. Then underline the word that best completes each sentence.

1. My body's (reflexes, response) happen so fast that I don't think about them.
2. All living things work to stay in balance, or maintain (equilibrium, stimulus).
3. (Reflexes, Senses) include sight, hearing, smell, taste, and touch.
4. Feeling hungry might be a (response, reflexes) to the smell of good food.
5. Bright sunlight is a (senses, stimulus) that might cause you to squint.

Name

FOR USE WITH PAGE 175

Skill Building

A. Use the Science Process Think about stimuli in your home, such as smells from the kitchen, the indoor temperature, and sounds outside the window. Write 3 possible stimuli in the first column below. In the second column, predict your response to each stimulus.

Stimulus: ***If***	**Response:** ***Then***

B. Writing Sentences Write 2–3 sentences telling how you might test your predictions.

Name

My Study Notes

A. Study Skill: Outlining the Lesson

Complete a study outline of this lesson. Use the headings in *ACCESS Science* to fill in the blanks.

1. Responding to the Inside Environment
   a. Balancing Temperature
   b.
   c.
   d.
2. Responding to the Outside Environment
   a.
   b. Reflexes
   c.
3.
   a. The First Defense
   b.
   c.

B. Key Facts

As you study the lesson, use the Word Bank to complete these sentences.

Word Bank
- nervous system
- infection
- immune system
- glands

1. Your ____________________ make chemicals and send them to other parts of your body that use them.

2. Your ____________________ is made up of your brain, spinal cord, nerves, and sense organs.

3. Your body's ____________________ protects it from germs and viruses.

4. When germs and viruses get into your body, they can cause ____________________.

Name ______________________

FOR USE WITH PAGE 182

Showing What I Know

A. Predicting Think about an outdoor activity or sport you enjoy. In the first box, draw a picture of a stimulus that might occur, such as the sounds and actions of other people or animals in the environment. In the second box, draw a picture to show how your body might respond to the stimulus.

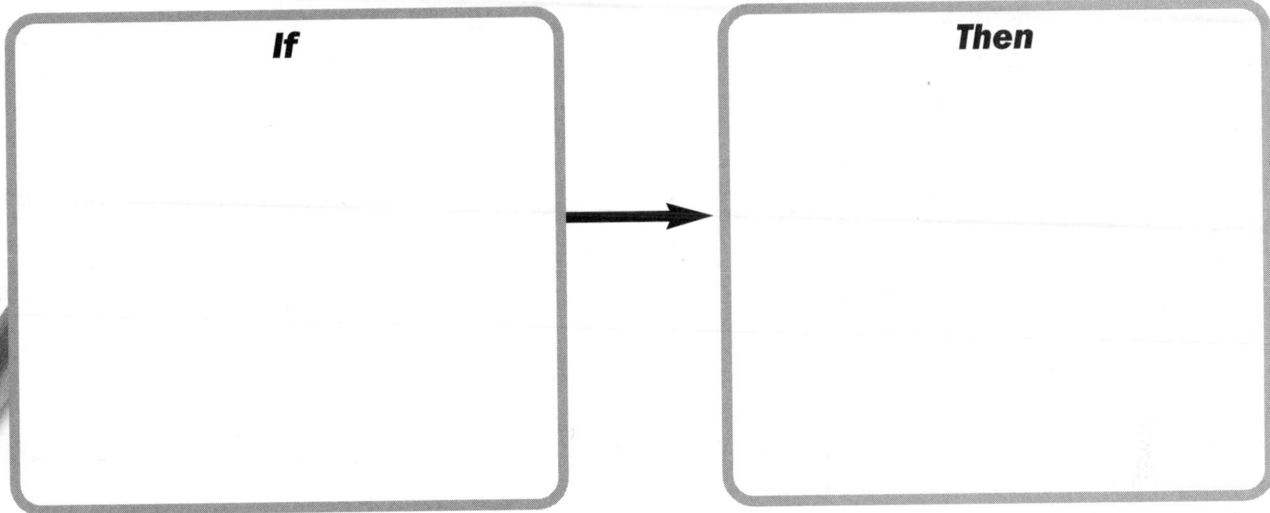

B. My Word Bank Write words on the lines below to describe your pictures. Then explain your prediction to a partner.

My Summary of the Lesson

Name

Reproduction and Inheritance

My Word List

A. Definition Web As you study the lesson, complete this Definition Web. Write a definition or an example sentence in each box.

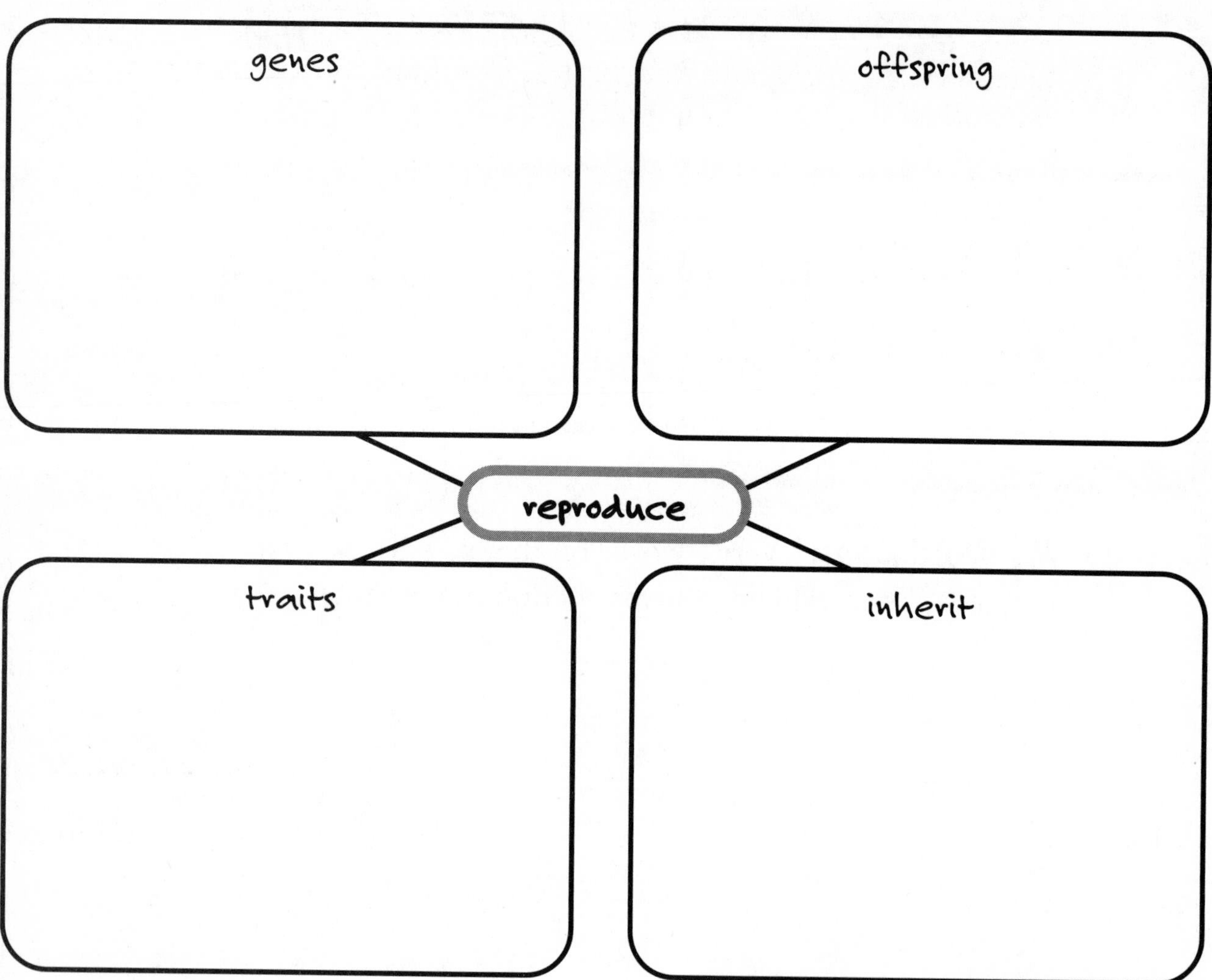

B. Sentence Frame Use the words in your Definition Web to complete the paragraph below.

Living things ________________ to create babies. Parents' babies are called their ________________. Each parent has chromosomes that carry ________________. These determine what ________________ the offspring will have. That's how children ________________ traits from their parents.

Name

FOR USE WITH PAGE 187

Skill Building

A. Look for Patterns In the box below, draw a picture of the people in your family or a family you know. Include brothers and sisters, parents, and grandparents. Show details such as hair and eye color. Then look at your picture. What traits do the family members have? Do you see a pattern?

B. My Word Bank First, use details from your picture to write the words you need to describe your pattern of family traits. Then, explain your pattern to a partner.

Name

My Study Notes

A. Study Skill: Using a Magnet Summary Complete a Magnet Summary for this lesson. Use headings in the book to fill in the detail boxes. Then write a short summary about the topic.

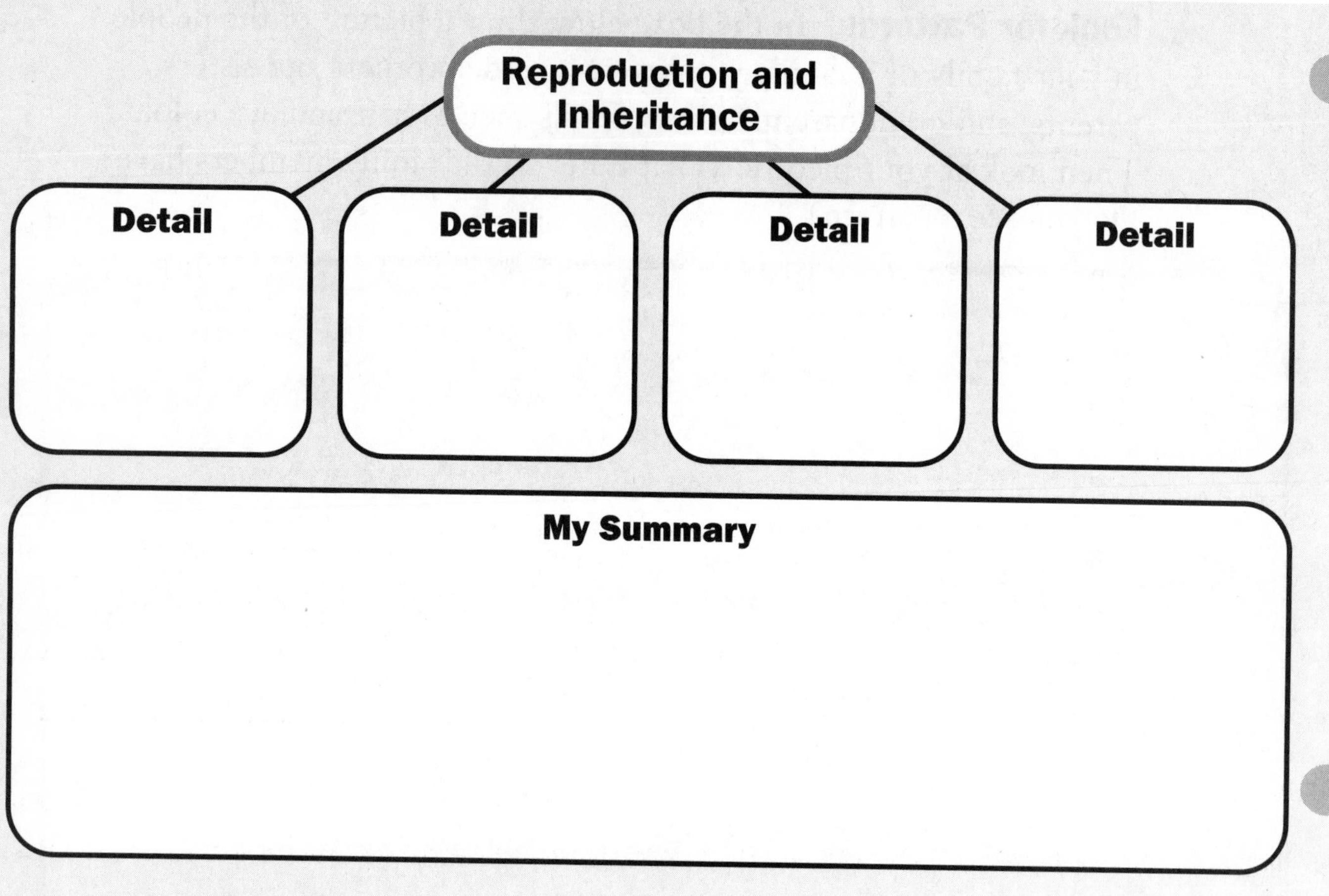

B. Key Facts Use the Word Bank to complete these sentences.

1. When there is only one parent, the offspring is produced ________________.

2. When two parents create offspring together, it is done through ________________ reproduction.

3. Sex cells are created in a process called ________________.

4. When a ________________ is present, the offspring will have the trait it carries.

5. An offspring can have a recessive trait only if it inherits a ________________ from each parent.

Word Bank
- meiosis
- recessive gene
- sexual
- dominant gene
- asexually

Name

FOR USE WITH PAGE 194

Showing What I Know

A. Describing In the Punnett squares below, B stands for the dominant gene of brown eyes and b stands for the recessive gene of blue eyes. Write letters in the squares on the left to show all the possible combinations. Then draw and color a picture of each child's eyes in the squares on the right.

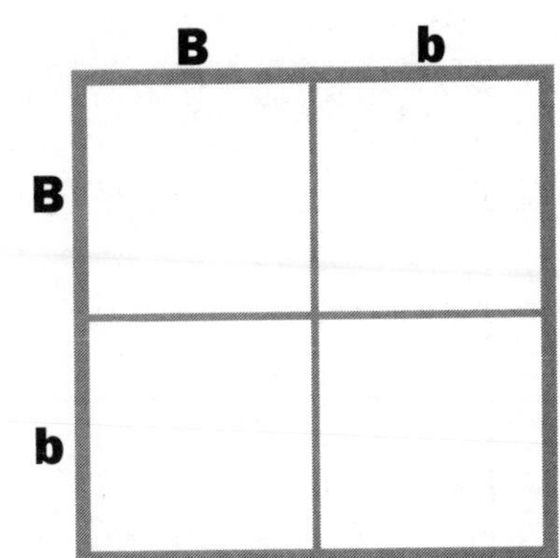

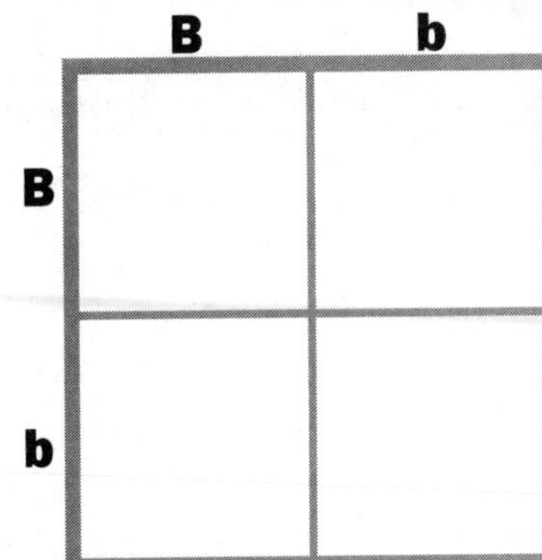

B. Writing Sentences Imagine that the parents Bb and Bb have 4 children, one for each square. What color eyes would most of their children have? Explain your answer in 2–3 sentences.

My Summary of the Lesson

Name

Change over Time

My Word List

A. Definition Chart Find these words in the lesson. Write the definition and use each word in a sentence.

Word	Definition	Example Sentence
adaptation		
advantage		
natural selection		
generations		
extinction		

B. Sentence Frame Use the words in your Definition Chart to complete the sentences below.

1. When bears developed the ______________ of sleeping during the winter, it helped the species survive.
2. Species that do not adapt to their environments over time may face ______________.
3. Changes in a species develop over many ______________.
4. Insects that blend into their environments can have an ______________ over insects that do not blend in.
5. The process of ______________________ is how adaptations pass to new generations of a species.

Name ______________________

FOR USE WITH PAGE 199

Skill Building

A. Identify Evidence After you read page 201 of *ACCESS Science*, complete this Evidence Organizer to support the hypothesis below. Write evidence that supports the hypothesis in the two boxes.

Hypothesis:

Walking stick insects have adaptations that help them survive in their environment.

Evidence:

Evidence:

B. Writing Sentences Use the details from your organizer to write 2–3 sentences explaining how your evidence supports the hypothesis.

Name

My Study Notes

A. Study Skill: Outlining the Lesson Complete a study outline of this lesson. Use the headings in *ACCESS Science* on pages 200–205 to fill in the outline.

1. Traits and Adaptations
   a. Changing Traits
   b.
2.
   a. Requirements for Survival
   b.
3. Evidence of Change
   a.
   b.

B. Key Facts Use the Word Bank to match each definition with the word it describes. Write the letter of the word on the line.

1. ____ Helpful adaptations can improve a species' chances of this.

2. ____ These remains give scientists clues about how species change.

3. ____ Examples include a parent, a grandparent, and a great-grandparent.

4. ____ A snake's tiny pelvis is one example of this.

5. ____ These are small differences among individuals of the same species.

6. ____ This verb describes how changes come about over time.

Word Bank

A. disappearing trait
B. survival
C. variations
D. fossils
E. develop
F. ancestor

Name

FOR USE WITH PAGE 206

Showing What I Know

Summarizing Draw pictures in the Evidence Organizer to support the hypothesis below. You can use the pictures on page 198 of *ACCESS Science* for clues. Then use your pictures to write a 2- or 3-sentence summary telling how they support the hypothesis.

Hypothesis:
Over time, giraffes adapted to the food source in their habitat.

Giraffes Then	Giraffes' Food Source	Giraffes Now

Summary:

My Summary of the Lesson

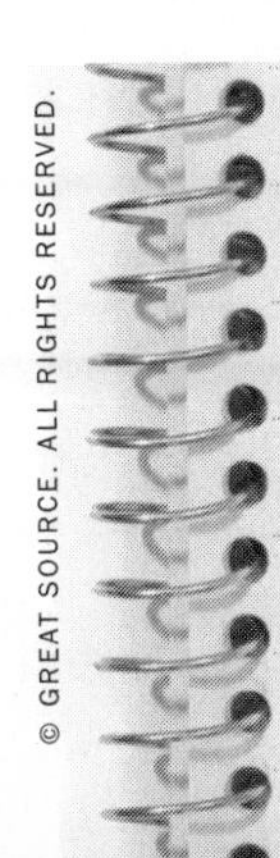

Name

The Structure of Matter

My Word List

A. Definition Web Write a definition for each word on the Definition Web. Use pages 210–213 of *ACCESS Science* for help.

mass:

volume:

matter

particles:

atoms:

B. Completing a Paragraph Use the words in your Definition Web to complete this paragraph.

Matter is anything that has ______________ and takes up space. Mass is measured in grams. ______________ is measured in cubic centimeters. All matter is made up of ______________. These building blocks of matter are made up of even smaller pieces called ______________.

Name ______________________

FOR USE WITH PAGE 211

Skill Building

A. Read a Model Read this model. Then use the information on pages 213–215 in *ACCESS Science* to write a caption for the model.

Iron (Fe)

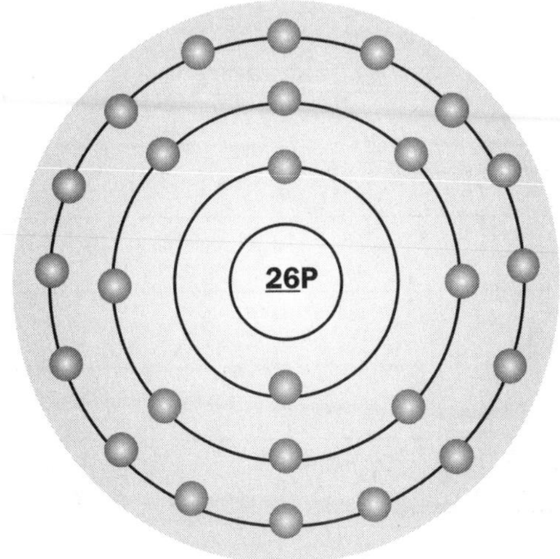

____

B. Writing Steps Review page 211 in *ACCESS Science*. What steps should you follow when reading a model? Write them here.

Step 1: ______________________

Step 2: ______________________

Step 3: ______________________

Step 4: ______________________

Name ____________________

My Study Notes

A. Study Skill: Key Word or Topic Notes Use the information on pages 215–217 of *ACCESS Science* to help you complete these Key Word or Topic Notes.

Key Words or Topics	Notes
element	
molecule	
compound	
mixture	

B. Key Facts As you study the lesson, use the Word Bank to answer these questions.

Word Bank
- protons
- electrons
- neutrons
- positive
- negative

1. What kind of charge do electrons have?

____

2. What particles make up the nucleus of an atom?

____________ and ____________

3. What kind of charge does the nucleus have?

____

4. What moves in clouds around the nucleus? ____________________

Name ______________________________

FOR USE WITH PAGE 218

Showing What I Know

A. Interpreting Look at the model of the atom below. Count the number of protons and electrons it has. Write the numbers on the lines. Think about what these numbers mean.

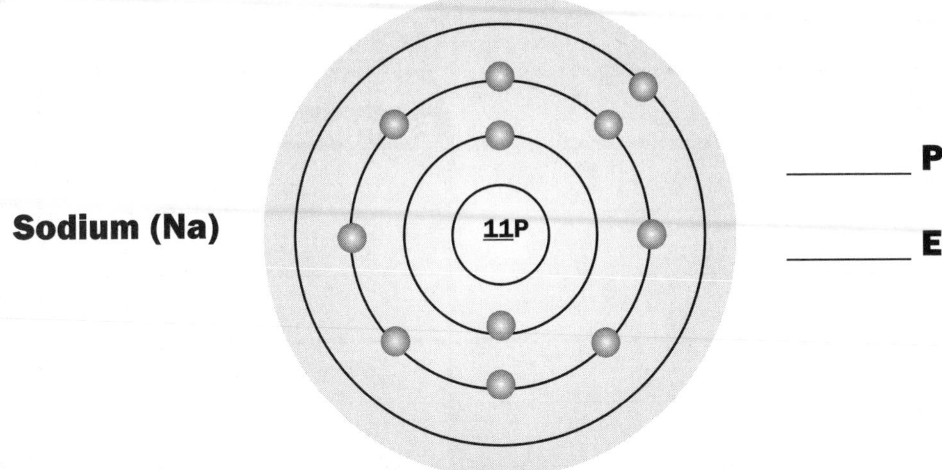

_______ P

_______ E

B. Writing an Interpretation In 2–3 sentences, tell what the model above means.

____

____

____

____

____

____

My Summary of the Lesson

Name

States of Matter

My Word List

A. Definition Chart Find these words in the lesson. Write the definition and use each word in a sentence.

Word	Definition	Examples
solid		
liquid		
gas		

B. Analyzing a Recipe Study the recipe ingredients below. Then make a check mark to show whether each ingredient is liquid or solid.

Ingredient	Liquid	Solid
cream		
mushrooms		
onion		
water		
salt		

Name

FOR USE WITH PAGE 223

Skill Building

A. Visualize Draw a picture that shows the 3 states of matter.

B. Writing Sentences Now write 2–3 sentences that say how your picture shows 3 different states of matter.

Name

My Study Notes

A. Study Skill: Main Idea Organizer Use what you've learned in the lesson to complete this organizer.

Main Idea: A change in the amount of thermal energy can cause matter to change from one state to another.

Detail	Detail	Detail

B. Key Facts After you study the lesson, choose the word from the Word Bank that matches each definition.

Word Bank
- weight
- temperature
- classify
- density
- condense

1. ________________: a measure of the average kinetic energy of a substance

2. ________________: the measure of the force of gravity on an object's mass

3. ________________: turn from a gas to a liquid

4. ________________: mass per unit volume

5. ________________: sort or organize by characteristics

Name

FOR USE WITH PAGE 230

Showing What I Know

Describing Complete these Summary Notes by describing each kind of change. Use pages 224–229 of *ACCESS Science* if you need help.

Topic: How matter can change state

Main Point: Matter can change state in 5 ways.

1. Solid to liquid:

2. Liquid to solid:

3. Liquid to gas:

4. Gas to liquid:

5. Solid to gas:

My Summary of the Lesson

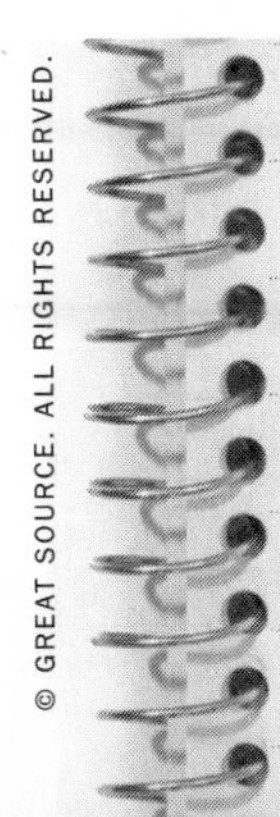

Name

Properties and the Periodic Table

My Word List

A. Word Match Match each vocabulary word in Column 1 to the most closely related meaning in Column 2. Put the letter of the best meaning in Column 2 on the line in Column 1.

Column 1	Column 2
element _____	A. unique
react _____	B. substance
nucleus _____	C. characteristics
stable _____	D. change
properties _____	E. center
distinctive _____	F. balanced

B. Writing Sentences Use some words from Column 1 above to write two sentences. The first sentence should explain the term *properties*, and the second sentence should tell about the periodic table.

Sentence 1 ______________________________

____

____

____

Sentence 2 ______________________________

____

____

____

Name

FOR USE WITH PAGE 235

Skill Building

A. Ask Questions Work with a partner. Each of you should choose a classroom object without telling the other what it is. Then think of yes/no questions you can ask your partner to figure out what object he or she chose. Write your questions below. Then ask your partner the questions. Answer your partner's questions.

B. Writing a Description Write a description of your partner's object. Tell as many of its properties as you can.

Name

My Study Notes

A. Study Skill: Making a Table

Use the periodic table (pages 238–239 in *ACCESS Science*) to complete this chart.

Element Name	Atomic Number	Chemical Symbol	Metal or Nonmetal?
copper			
potassium			
calcium			
helium			
radon			

B. Key Facts

After you study the lesson, use what you learned to answer these questions. Use pages 236–241 in *ACCESS Science* if you need help.

1. What is the name of the chart that organizes elements by their properties?

2. What are two examples of noble gases (Group 18)?

3. What are two radioactive elements?

4. Which group of elements are the best conductors?

5. Which elements are in Period 1?

Name

FOR USE WITH PAGE 242

Showing What I Know

Classifying Write properties of each group on the chart. Then give one example of each.

Classification

Metals	Metalloids	Nonmetals
Example:	**Example:**	**Example:**

My Summary of the Lesson

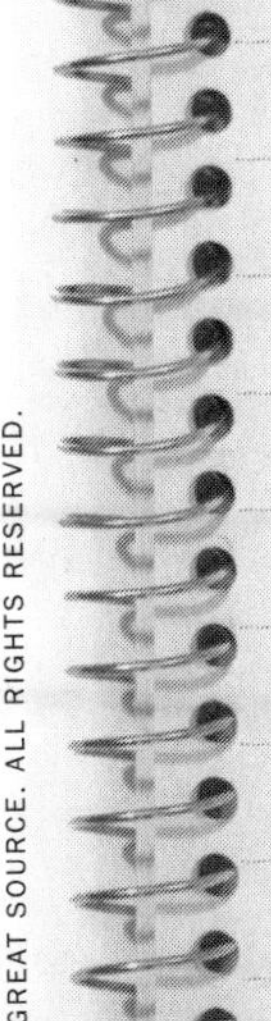

Name

Bonds, Reactions, and Energy

My Word List

A. Paraphrasing Definitions Look in *ACCESS Science* for the definitions of the terms in Column 1. Then write the definitions in your own words.

Word	Definition
reactant	
product	
energy	
compound	
dissolving	
kinetic energy	

B. Writing a Definition After you study the lesson, use the terms *atoms* and *electrons* in your own definition of a *covalent bond.* Then draw a picture of a covalent bond.

A covalent bond is	My picture

Name ____________________

FOR USE WITH PAGE 247

Skill Building

A. Infer from Evidence Reread page 247 in *ACCESS Science*. Visualize a cook cracking open an egg and pouring its contents into a hot pan. Then complete this chart.

Changes I Observe	What I Already Know	My Inferences About What Happens

B. Making Notes In the boxes, write clues—evidence—that can help you detect a chemical change.

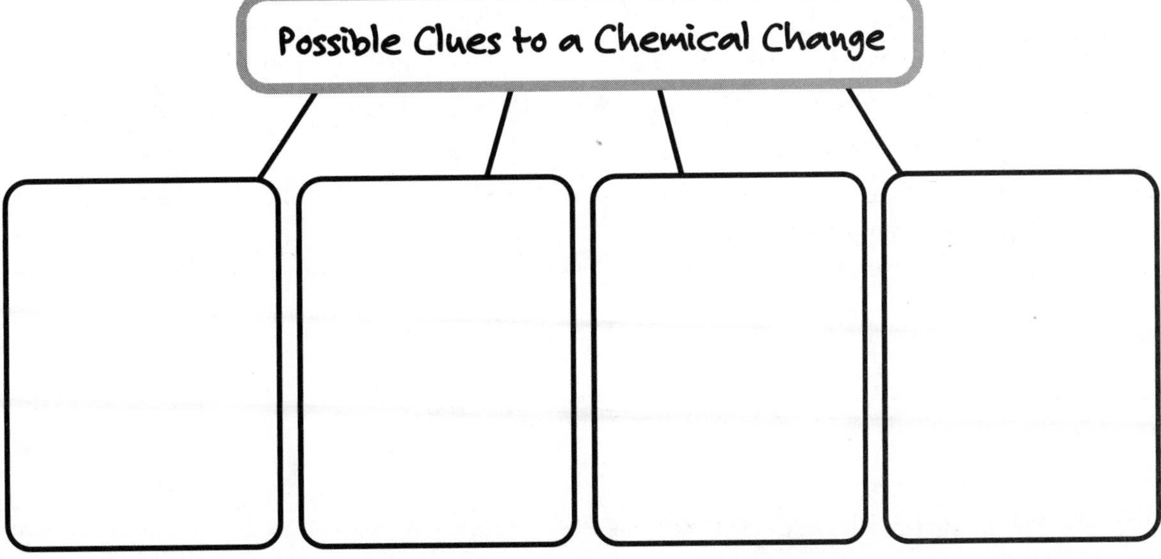

Name

FOR USE WITH PAGES 248–253

My Study Notes

A. Study Skill: Outlining the Lesson

Complete a study outline of Lesson 20. Use the headings in *ACCESS Science* to fill in the blanks.

1. Forming Bonds
   - a. Covalent Bonds
   - b. ______
   - c. ______
2. Chemical Reactions
   - a. ______
   - b. ______
   - c. ______
3. ______
   - a. Thermal Energy and Reactions
   - b. ______

B. Key Facts

As you study the lesson, use the Word Bank to complete these sentences.

1. Reactions that release ______ are exothermic.
2. Atoms that have a charge are called ______.
3. You can write an ______ to show a chemical reaction.
4. When two or more elements combine, the result can be a molecule or a ______.

Word Bank

- ions
- equation
- compound
- thermal energy

Name

FOR USE WITH PAGE 254

Showing What I Know

Explaining Below is an equation for the formation of glucose (sugar). Read it several times and then use the chart to explain the equation in your own words.

Equation:	$6\ CO_2$	+	$6\ H_2O$	$\longrightarrow$	$C_6H_{12}O_6$	+	$6\ O_2$
Explanation words							
Explanation sentence:							

Use the formula for glucose to explain conservation of mass.

My Summary of the Lesson

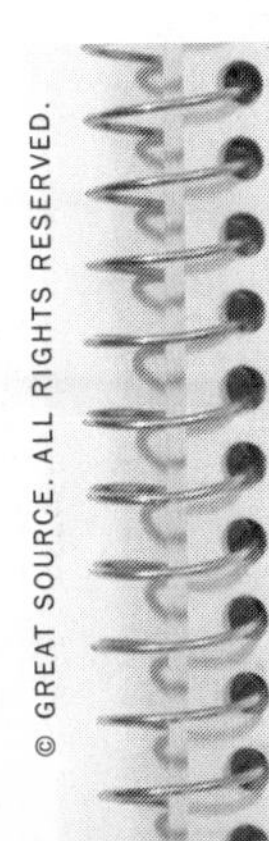

Name

Understanding Energy

My Word List

A. Writing Sentences After you study the lesson, use each word below in a sentence about energy.

Word	My Sentence
heat	
radiation	
appliance	
forms	
motion	

B. Illustrating a Concept Visualize a game you like to play outdoors. Then in the first box, draw a picture that shows one or more players with potential energy. In the second box, draw a picture that shows one or more players using kinetic energy.

Potential energy	Kinetic energy

Name

FOR USE WITH PAGE 259

Skill Building

A. Think About Systems Think about standing in a line to get lunch. Assume that this is a system. Read these individual parts of the system. Then put them in an order that makes sense.

Lunch Line System

- Cafeteria workers put food on trays.
- Students make their choices.
- Students pick up their trays.
- Students pay at the cash register.
- Students line up.

1.
2.
3.
4.
5.

B. Writing Sentences Study the lesson in *ACCESS Science*. Then on the lines below, write 4–6 sentences that tell some ways energy affects parts of the lunch line system.

Name

My Study Notes

A. Study Skill: Summary Notes As you study the lesson in *ACCESS Science*, complete these Summary Notes. First, read the topic and the main idea. Then, write 4 details that support the main idea.

Topic: Energy

Main Idea: Energy can change from one form to another.

1.

2.

3.

4.

B. Key Facts Use the Word Bank to match each definition with the word or concept it describes. Then write the letter on the line. You will not use all the letters.

1. _____ This noun means different kinds.

2. _____ The movement of energy through moving liquid or gas

3. _____ Potential and kinetic energy combined

4. _____ Changes from one kind to another

5. _____ An increase in this warms a room.

Word Bank

A. transforms
B. thermal energy
C. motion
D. forms
E. mechanical energy
F. convection

Name ______________________

FOR USE WITH PAGE 266

Showing What I Know

A. Relating Imagine writing a report on electricity as a system. On the Web below, place the steps in the ovals in order. Explain how each step in the system relates to the next step. Draw arrows to show the sequence.

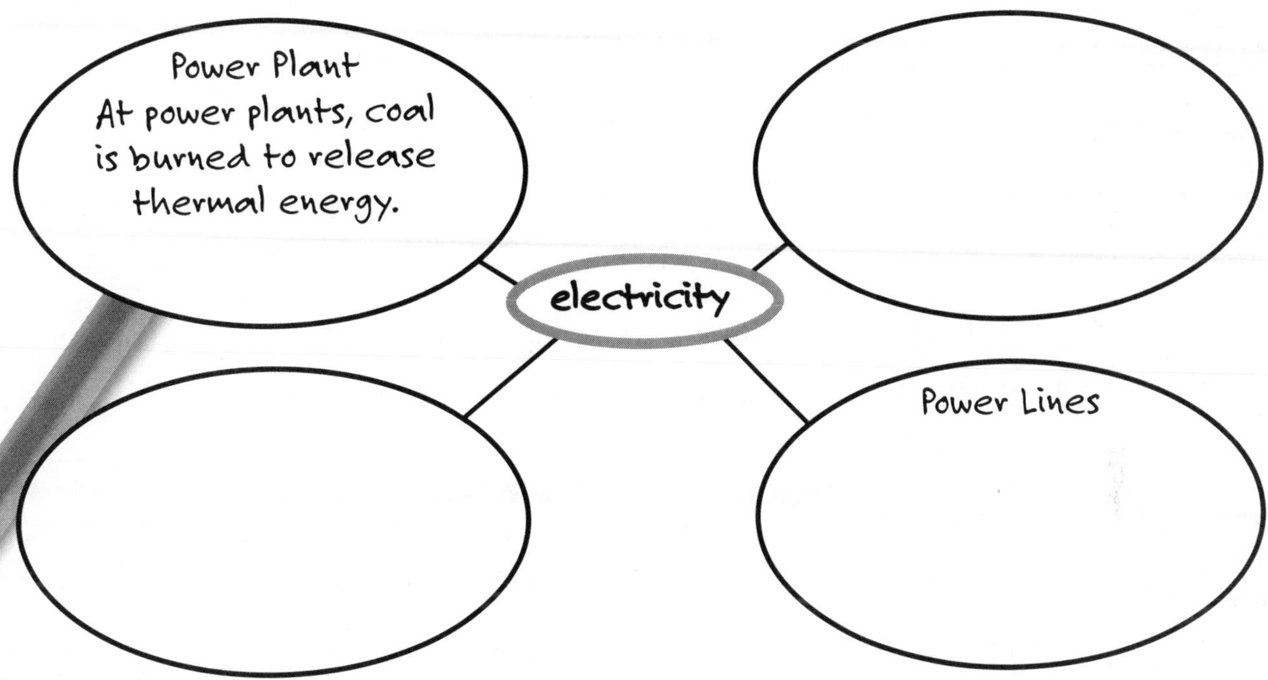

B. Writing a Paragraph Write a paragraph that relates the parts of electricity as a system. Pretend you are giving instructions to a new student.

____

____

____

____

My Summary of the Lesson

Name ____________________

Force and Motion

My Word List

A. Defining Terms After you study the lesson, write a definition for each word below.

velocity ____________________

distance ____________________

acceleration ____________________

B. Summarizing Data Below are data about a roller coaster in Great Heights Park. Study the data, and then summarize how the ride works using the words *velocity*, *distance*, and *acceleration*.

Roller Coaster: Thrill Rider	
Length	2,700 feet
Height	420 feet
Drop	380 feet
Speed	120 mph
Acceleration	0 to 120 mph in 4 seconds

____

____

____

____

____

____

____

____

Name

FOR USE WITH PAGE 271

Skill Building

A. Ask Questions Look at the picture at the top of page 274 in *ACCESS Science* and read the caption. Then imagine you are going to interview a skydiver. What questions would you like to ask? Write 4 questions that relate to the lesson.

Skydiving Questions

1.

2.

3.

4.

B. Science Questions After you study the lesson, write 2–4 questions about gravity and friction that you might be able to answer with an experiment.

Name

My Study Notes

A. Study Skill: Visualizing Choose one of Newton's 3 laws of motion on pages 276–277 in *ACCESS Science* and write it on the lines. Then draw and label a picture that shows the law at work.

B. Key Facts As you study the lesson, list examples in each column of this chart.

Force	Motion

Name

FOR USE WITH PAGE 278

Showing What I Know

Predicting Use what you know about Newton's Second Law to predict what will happen when you hit a baseball with a bat. Use the Prediction Organizer below.

Observations	My Prediction

Write 2–3 sentences that explain your prediction.

My Summary of the Lesson

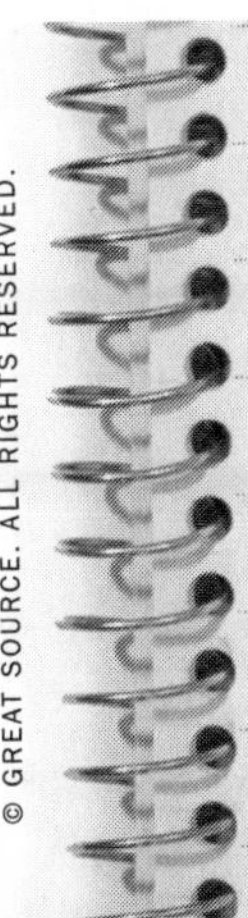

Name ______________________________

Light and Sound

My Word List

A. Understanding Key Concepts Complete this Web. Define each word and then write a sentence that explains how the word relates to light and sound.

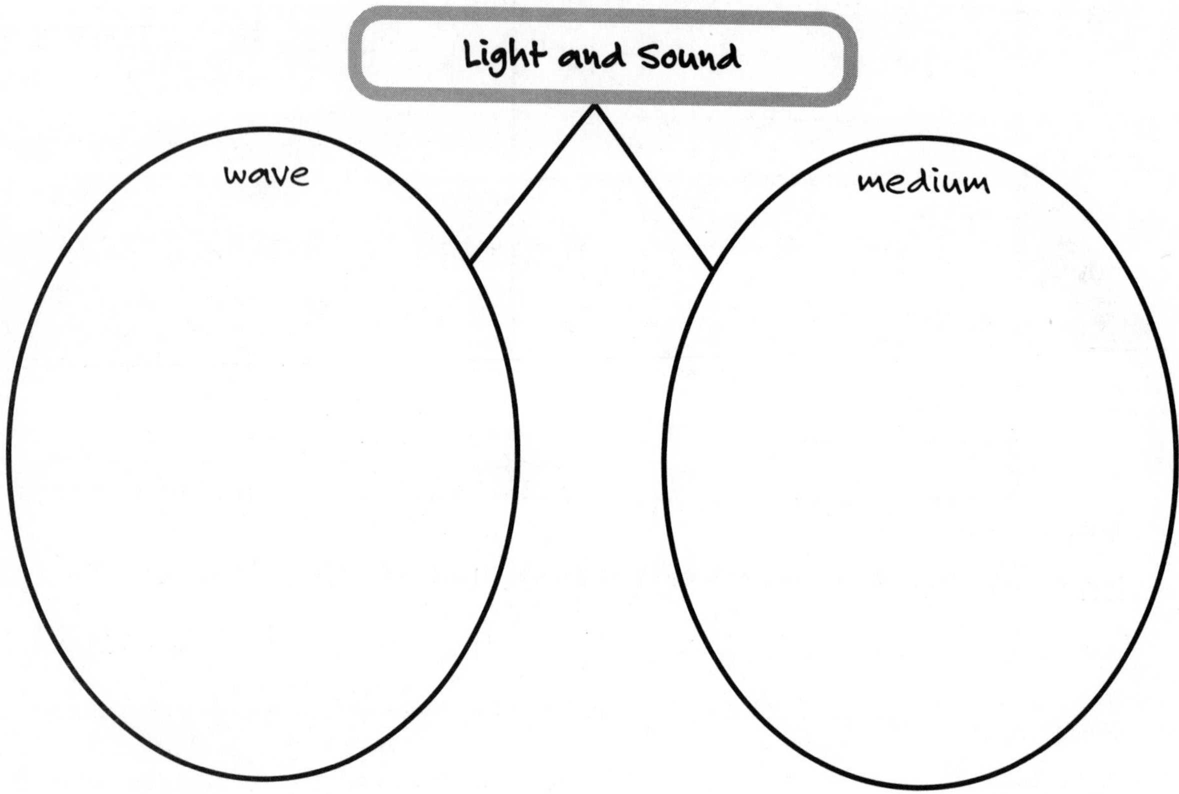

B. Writing Sentences Study the Eyes and Ears illustration at the bottom of pages 282–283 of *ACCESS Science.* Then write 4–6 sentences to explain how our eyes detect light and our ears detect sound.

____

____

____

____

____

____

Name ______________________________ FOR USE WITH PAGE 283

Skill Building

A. Use Math Use math to answer these questions. Show your work.

1. If light travels at the speed of about 300,000 kilometers per second, how many kilometers does it travel in a half hour?

____

____

____

2. How many kilometers does it travel in an hour?

____

____

____

3. The average distance from Earth to the moon is 384,400 kilometers. How long does it take for light to go from Earth to the moon?

____

____

____

B. Writing Sentences Use the lines below to write 2–3 sentences that describe the speed of light. Use adjectives and one of the examples above.

____

____

____

____

____

____

____

Name

My Study Notes

A. Study Skill: Using a Diagram

After you study Lesson 23 in *ACCESS Science*, label parts of this diagram using words from the Word Bank below.

Word Bank

crest

trough

amplitude

wavelength

B. Key Facts

Study the lesson. Then draw a line between each word in Column A and the best definition of the word in Column B.

Column A	Column B
reflects •	• a coil of metal
medium •	• throws back
pitch •	• the highness or lowness of sound
spring •	• the force of sound
loudness •	• the substance through which something moves

Name

FOR USE WITH PAGE 290

Showing What I Know

A. Summarizing Use information from Lesson 23 in *ACCESS Science* to fill in the chart.

Topic	Main Ideas	Summary
Light waves	• Light waves are called electromagnetic waves.	

B. Main Ideas Write three main ideas from the lesson. Then use the list to help as you write your summary of the lesson.

1.

2.

3.

My Summary of the Lesson

Name

Matter in the Universe

My Word List

A. Understanding Vocabulary After you study the lesson, write 2–3 sentences that explain how these three words relate to each other.

astronomers	galaxies	universe

B. Writing a Want Ad Imagine you need to hire an astronomer for a new project. Write an advertisement that tells about the job (a "want ad"). See how many words from the lesson you can use.

Name ____________________ FOR USE WITH PAGE 295

Skill Building

A. Analyze Data After you study page 295 in *ACCESS Science*, use what you learned to analyze these data. First, read the chart. Then, use a complete sentence to answer each question.

Planet	Distance from the Sun
Pluto	5,916,000,000 km
Mercury	57,900,000 km

Approximately how many times closer is Mercury to the sun than Pluto?

____

How did you find the answer? ______________________________

B. Comparing Data Study the data in the chart below. Then compare the diameters and densities of the two planets.

Planet	Diameter	Density
Venus	12,104 km	5.24 g/cm^3
Mars	6,796 km	3.93 g/cm^3

My Comparisons:

____

____

____

____

____

Name

My Study Notes

A. Study Skill: Key Word or Topic Notes As you study Lesson 24 in *ACCESS Science*, complete this chart. Make notes about the following key words or topics.

Key Words or Topics	Notes
universe	contains all matter and energy
stars	held together by gravity
solar system	

B. Picture Dictionary Define these two terms. Then draw a picture of an example of each.

gas giant:

terrestrial planet:

Name

FOR USE WITH PAGE 302

Showing What I Know

A. Comparing and Contrasting Read the data in the chart below. Then use the Venn Diagram to compare and contrast the two planets.

Planet	Distance from the sun	Number of Moons	Rings?	Diameter
Jupiter	778,330,000 km	60	yes	142,800 km
Saturn	1,429,400,000 km	31	yes	120,000 km

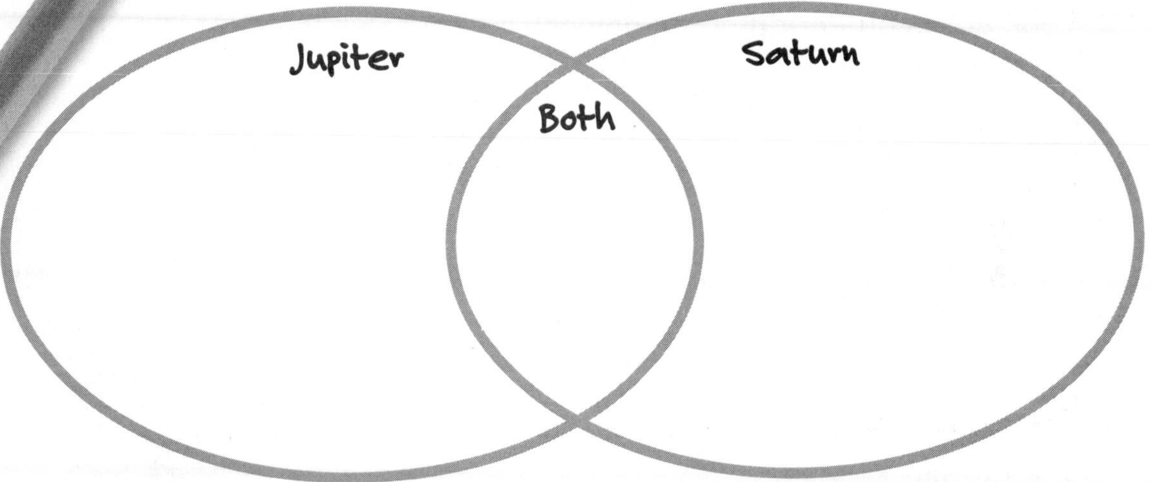

B. Writing Sentences Write 3 sentences that compare and contrast Jupiter and Saturn.

My Summary of the Lesson

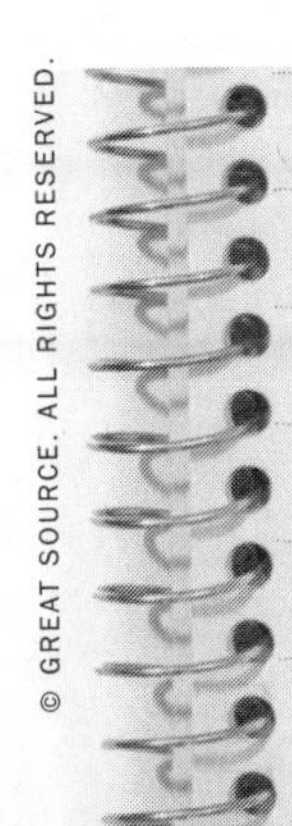

References

How to Measure with a Meterstick

You use a meterstick to measure length. A meterstick is one meter long. It is divided into 100 centimeters. Each centimeter is further divided into ten smaller units called millimeters. You can use all of these units on the meterstick to measure length.

1. Line up the "0" end of the meterstick with one end of the object you are measuring.
2. Look at the other end of the object. Observe how long the object is in centimeters and millimeters.
3. This pencil is 17 centimeters plus 5 millimeters long. You can write this length as 17.5 centimeters.

How do you measure the length of something that is longer than a meter, such as a wall?

1. Line up the "0" end of the meterstick with the end of the wall.
2. Make a light mark on the wall or hold your finger at the other end of the meterstick.
3. Move the meterstick so that the "0" end lines up with the mark or with your finger. Be sure to keep the stick level.
4. Continue to move and mark lengths of the meterstick until you reach the end of the wall. Then add up all the measurements. For example, the wall might be 5 meters and 25 centimeters, or 5.25 meters, long.

How to Measure Volume

Volume of a Liquid

The amount of space something takes up is its volume. The water in the large glass takes up more space than the water in the small glass. The pitcher holds a larger volume of water. How much more? You have to measure to find out. In science, you measure volume by using beakers, graduated cylinders, and metric measuring cups. These containers usually are marked in milliliters (mL). The most accurate measuring container is a graduated cylinder.

1. Look at the graduated cylinder. It is marked with 100 mL. Every tenth milliliter is labeled.
2. Pour the liquid you are measuring into a graduated cylinder. Notice that the surface of the water in the cylinder curves up at the sides. You measure the volume by reading the height of the water at the lowest part of the curve. The water shown in the graduated cylinder in the picture has a volume of 65 mL.

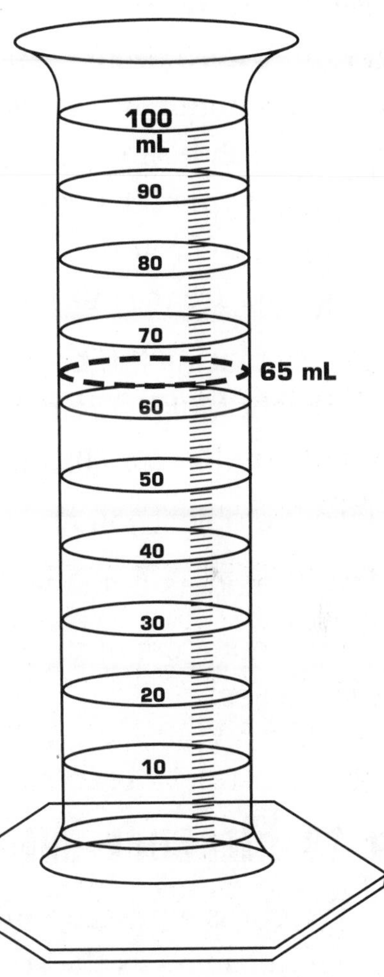

Volume of a Box

All matter has volume. You can find the volume of a box by multiplying its length by its width by its height. The volume is measured in cubic centimeters (cm^3).

volume = length × width × height

= 6 cm × 3 cm × 2 cm

= 36 cm^3

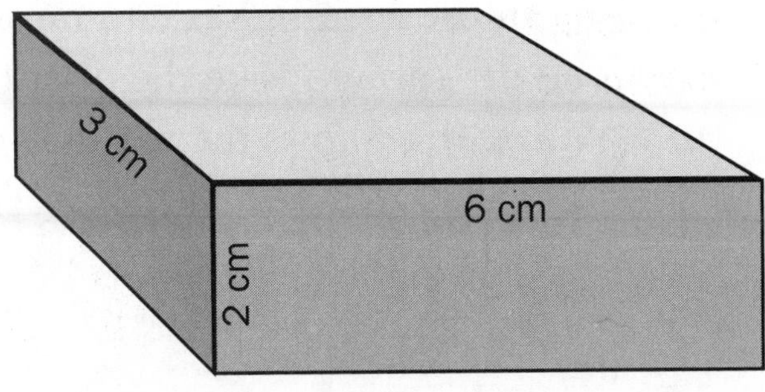

How to Measure Mass

You can use a balance to measure mass in grams. There are different kinds of balances. One kind is a triple-beam balance. It has three bars, or beams. One beam measures single grams. Another beam measures tens of grams. A third beam measures hundreds of grams. Each beam has a weight, or rider, that you can move to balance the object you are measuring.

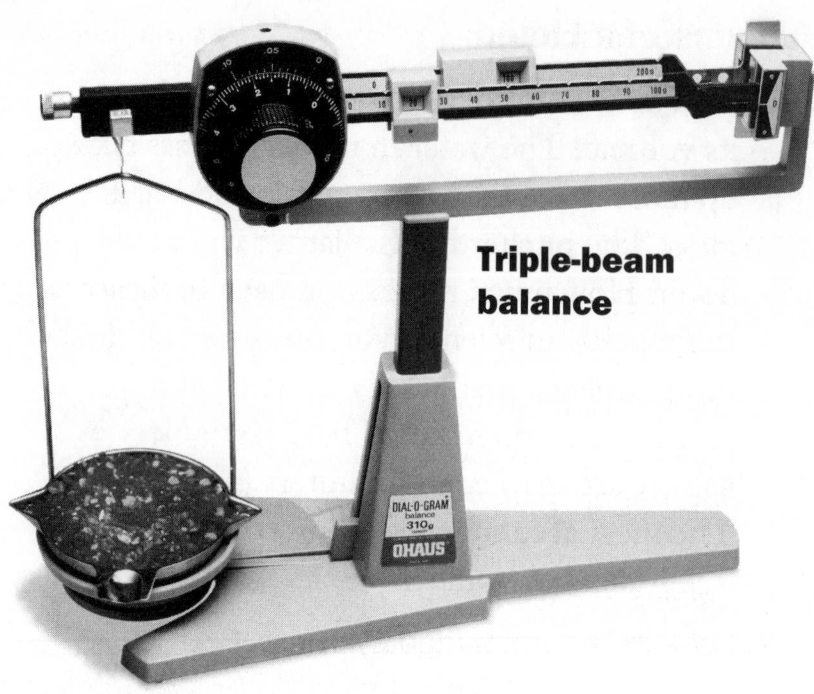

Triple-beam balance

1. Start by placing the balance on a level surface. Move the riders all the way to the left. Make sure the pointer points to the zero mark. If it does not, slowly turn the zeroing screw until the pointer is at zero.
2. Place the object you are measuring onto the balance pan.
3. Move the riders until the pointer once again points to the zero mark.
4. Add the numbers of the readings for all three beams. The total is the mass of the object.

How to Measure Weight

Weight is a measure of the force of gravity on an object's mass. Weight changes as the strength of gravity changes.

You can use a spring scale to measure weight. The object pulls down on the spring inside the plastic tube. The spring is connected to a pointer that shows the weight in newtons (N).

How to Measure Temperature

Temperature is a measure of thermal energy. You measure temperature with a thermometer.

A thermometer is a narrow tube that contains colored liquid. When a liquid gets warmer, it gains energy. The particles of liquid move farther apart. That makes the liquid rise in the tube. When the liquid gets cooler, it loses energy. The particles move closer together, and the liquid falls in the tube.

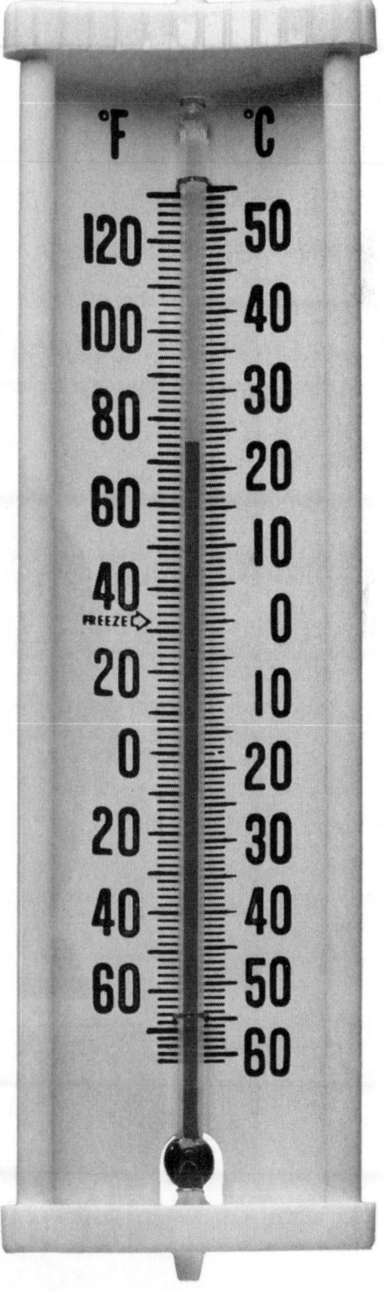

1. Look at the thermometer. Notice what scale it uses. The thermometer might use the Fahrenheit scale and measure temperature in degrees Fahrenheit (°F). It might use the Celsius scale and measure in degrees Celsius (°C).
2. Place the thermometer so that the bottom part, or bulb, is in the material you are measuring. For example, when measuring the temperature of water, make sure the bulb is in the water.
3. Wait until the liquid in the thermometer stops moving. This may take a minute or two.
4. Read the number next to the top of the colored liquid. Make sure you know how many degrees each mark on the scale stands for. The temperature shown on this thermometer is 75 °F (23.5 °C).

How to Use a Magnifying Glass

A magnifying glass is a tool that magnifies an object, or makes the object look bigger. You use a magnifying glass to see details that would be difficult to see without the glass. You might use a magnifying glass to see the shape of a grain of salt. You could use a magnifying glass to observe the legs of an ant or pollen on a flower.

1. Hold the magnifying glass a few centimeters from the object. Move the magnifying glass toward or away from the object until its edges are easy to see.
2. Some magnifying glasses have more than one lens. If your magnifying glass has two lenses, look at the object through the larger lens first.
3. Then look at the object through the smaller lens. This lens is more powerful, so you will be able to see even more detail. You may have to move the magnifying glass forward or away again to see the object clearly.

How to Use a Microscope

A microscope can make an object look hundreds of times larger. Students often use a kind of microscope called a compound microscope. It has different kinds of lenses.

1. Place the microscope on a flat surface. If you have to carry the microscope, use both hands. Hold the arm of the microscope with one hand and support the base with your other hand.
2. Look at the picture to learn the different parts of the microscope. Take time to find these parts on the microscope you are using.
3. Position the mirror so that it reflects light up toward the stage. Look through the eyepiece. Move the lever of the diaphragm so that the light shines through the opening in the stage.
4. Place a prepared slide on the stage so that the specimen is over the center of the opening. Put the slide under the stage clips to hold the slide in place.
5. Look at the microscope from the side. Turn the coarse adjustment knob to lower the body tube. Lower the tube until the low-power objective almost touches the slide. Do not let the objective touch the slide.
6. Look through the eyepiece. If the object looks blurry, use the coarse adjustment knob to raise the body tube. Make the object appear as clear as you can.
7. Use the fine adjustment knob to make the object appear even more clearly.
8. To change magnification, turn the nosepiece until the high-power objective clicks in place. Then use the fine adjustment knob to make the object appear clearly.

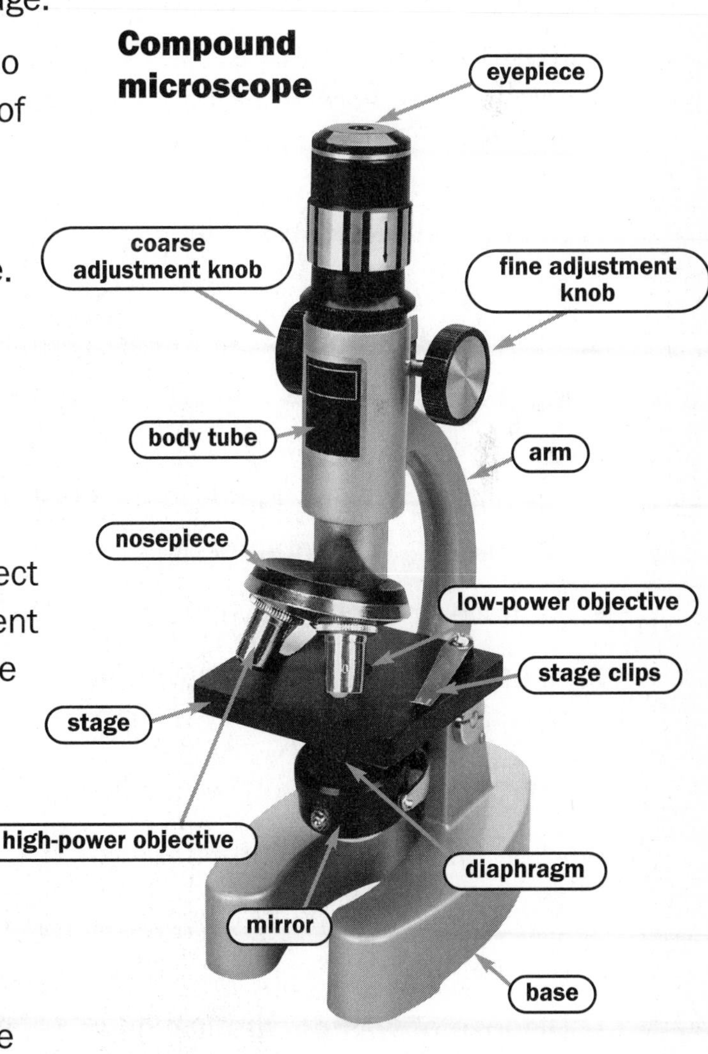

Lab Safety

Read these safety rules before doing any science experiment. Ask your teacher to explain any rules you do not understand.

General Safety

1. Read all of the instructions for an experiment carefully. Ask your teacher to explain any instructions you do not understand. Look for safety symbols and warnings.
2. Never eat or drink in the laboratory.
3. Wear safety goggles when working with chemicals, glassware, flames, or any material that might get in your eyes.
4. Wear a lab apron.
5. Tie back long hair and secure loose clothing to keep it away from flames, chemicals, and equipment.
6. Remove or secure jewelry so that it does not dangle.
7. Keep your work area uncluttered. Keep backpacks and books away from equipment.
8. Get permission from the teacher before beginning any experiment.
9. Wipe up any spills immediately.
10. After the experiment, clean your work area. Return all equipment to its proper place.
11. Dispose of waste materials as your teacher tells you.
12. Wash your hands before leaving the lab.

Heating and Electrical Safety

1. Never heat anything without your teacher's permission.
2. Never reach across an open flame.
3. Keep any material that can burn, such as nail polish remover, away from flames.
4. Never leave a lighted burner or a hot plate unattended.
5. When you are heating a substance in a test tube, point the test tube opening away from yourself and others.
6. Do not heat a liquid in a closed container.
7. Do not touch a burner or hot plate right after you turn it off. It will still be hot. Do not use your bare hands to pick up a container that has just been heated. Find out if it is still hot by holding the back of your hand near it. If you feel heat, use an oven mitt or tongs to pick up the container.
8. Never use a piece of electrical equipment that has a frayed cord or an exposed wire.

Chemical Safety

1. Never mix chemicals just to see what happens. Some chemicals that are harmless separately can explode when combined.
2. Do not touch, taste, or smell a chemical unless your teacher tells you to do so. If you are instructed to smell a chemical, use a hand motion to waft the odors toward your nose. Never inhale fumes directly from a container.
3. When mixing an acid and water, add the acid to the water. Never add water to the acid—it will splatter.
4. If you spill or splash a chemical, tell your teacher immediately.

Glassware Safety

1. Check to make sure heated glassware has cooled before you pick it up with bare hands.
2. Do not eat or drink from lab glassware.
3. Never use broken or chipped glassware, such as chipped microscope slides, beakers, or test tubes.
4. Tell your teacher if glassware breaks. Follow directions for disposing of the broken glassware. Do not handle it with your bare hands.

Safety with Sharp Objects

1. Handle sharp tools, such as scalpels, knives, pins, and scissors, carefully. Cut by moving the sharp edge away from your body, not toward your body.
2. Tell your teacher if you or someone else gets cut.
3. Cover the edges of cans and other sharp edges with tape.

Plant and Animal Safety

1. Tell your teacher if you are allergic to any plants or animals.
2. Handle plants or animals as your teacher tells you.
3. Do not taste any part of a plant.
4. Never perform an experiment that will harm an animal.
5. If you keep animals to observe in the lab, learn how to care for them. Keep their homes clean. Give them enough food, water, and space.
6. Wash your hands after handling animals and their cages or tanks. Wash your hands after handling plants or soil.